Outstanding Dissertations in
LINGUISTICS

edited by
LAURENCE HORN
Yale University

CLAUSES WITHOUT "THAT"

THE CASE FOR BARE SENTENTIAL COMPLEMENTATION IN ENGLISH

CATHAL DOHERTY

Routledge
Taylor & Francis Group
LONDON AND NEW YORK

First Published 2000 by
Garland Publishing Inc.

Published 2013 by Routledge
2 Park Square, Milton Park, Abingdon, Oxfordshire OX14 4RN
711 Third Avenue, New York, NY 10017

Routledge is an imprint of the Taylor and Francis Group, an informa business

First issued in paperback 2015

Copyright © 2000 by Cathal Doherty

All rights reserved. No part of this book may be reprinted or reproduced or utilized in any form or by any electronic, mechanical, or other means, now known or hereafter invented, including photocopying and recording, or in any information storage or retrieval system, without permission in writing from the publishers.

Library of Congress Cataloging-in-Publication Data
Doherty, Cathal.
    Clauses without "that": the case for bare sentential complementation in English / Cathal Doherty.
        p. cm. — (Outstanding dissertations in linguistics)
    Includes bibliographical references and index.
    ISBN 978-0-8153-3775-1 (hbk)
    ISBN 978-1-138-99139-2 (pbk)
    1. English language—Complement. 2. English language—Clauses.
I. Title. II. Series.
PE1385.D64 2000
425—dc21   00-026132
ISBN   978-0-815-33775-1 (hbk)

For B. and N. Doherty (Fintan)

Contents

PREFACE xi

ACKNOWLEDGEMENTS xiii

Chapter 1: The Category of *That*-less clauses 3
   1. CLAUSE STRUCTURE 3
   2. A QUESTION 5
      2.1. An Answer: the CP-Hypothesis 5
      2.2. An Answer: the IP-Hypothesis 7
   3. Outline of the Work 8
NOTES 10

Chapter 2 Argument Clauses 11
   1. INTRODUCTION 11
   2. ARGUMENTS FOR THE IP-HYPOTHESIS 12
      2.1. Embedded Topicalization 12
      2.2. Adverbial Adjunction 15
      2.3. Adjunction Evidence: Summary 17
   3. THE ECP ACCOUNT OF THE DISTRIBUTION OF *THAT*-LESS CLAUSES 18
      3.1. The Government Requirement 19
      3.2. Explaining the Government Requirement 20
         3.2.1. C^0 to V^0 Incorporation 20
         3.2.2. Head Government at Phonological Form 24
         3.2.3. Conclusion 27
      3.3. Empirical Problems 27
         3.3.1. Embedded Sentential Subjects 27
         3.3.2. Ungoverned Null Complementizers 31
      3.4. Summary 33

4. EXPLAINING THE DISTRIBUTION OF IP ... 33
   4.1. Previous Accounts: Webelhuth 1992 ... 34
   4.2. A Proposal ... 38
5. CHAPTER SUMMARY ... 40
6. APPENDIX: LEXICAL RESTRICTIONS ... 41
   6.1. Paradox: Selected Adjunct Clauses ... 42
   6.2. A Resolution ... 44
   6.3. Noun Complement Clauses ... 48
NOTES ... 50

CHAPTER 3 Relative Clauses ... 57
1. INTRODUCTION ... 57
   1.1. Syntactic Properties of Contact Clauses ... 59
   1.2. Restrictive Relative Clauses: Assumptions ... 61
2. THE STRUCTURE OF CONTACT CLAUSES ... 62
   2.1. Contact Clauses are IP ... 62
   2.2. The A´-Chain in Contact Clauses ... 64
      2.2.1. The Null Operator Approach ... 65
      2.2.2. Proposal: A´-Chains without Movement ... 66
   2.3. The Adjacency Restriction ... 67
   2.4. Summary ... 70
3. SUBJECT CONTACT CLAUSES ... 71
   3.1. Distribution: The Majority Dialect ... 72
   3.2. Subject Contact Clauses as non-Relative Clauses ... 73
      3.2.1. Independent Evidence for the Pseudo-Relative ... 75
      3.2.2. Subject Contact Clauses as Pseudo-Relatives ... 77
   3.3. Subject Contact Clauses are Relative Clauses ... 81
   3.4. Distribution: Liberal Dialects ... 87
   3.5. Summary ... 89
4. EXPLAINING THE DISTRIBUTION OF SUBJECT CONTACT CLAUSES ... 89
   4.1. Previous Accounts ... 90
      4.1.1. Pragmatic Accounts ... 90
      4.1.2. Non-Referentiality ... 91
   4.2. The Distribution of Post-Nominal Modifiers ... 92
5. CHAPTER SUMMARY ... 95
NOTES ... 95

CHAPTER 4 Extraction Theory 103
  1. INTRODUCTION 103
  2. THE *THAT*-TRACE EFFECT 104
  3. PREVIOUS ACCOUNTS 106
    3.1. Locality 107
      3.1.1. Locality as Binding 107
      3.1.2. Locality as Antecedent Government 108
    3.2. The Head-Government Account 110
      3.2.1. Agreement in Comp 112
      3.2.2. Advantages of the Account 113
      3.2.3. Some difficulties 114
  4. IMPLICATIONS FOR HEAD-GOVERNMENT 115
    4.1. Null Complementizers are Inert for Government 117
    4.2. Vacuous Movement 118
  5. CHAPTER SUMMARY 121
NOTES 122

CHAPTER 5 Concluding Remarks 125
  1. INTRODUCTION 125
  2. DISTRIBUTION OF NON-ROOT IP 126
  3. EXTENSION TO BARE INFINITIVES 127
NOTES 130

BIBLIOGRAPHY 131

INDEX 139

Preface

This book is a slightly revised version of my Ph.D. dissertation which was submitted on 10 December 1993 at the University of California, Santa Cruz. The committee members were Jim McCloskey (chair), Sandra Chung, Donka Farkas and Bill Ladusaw. In preparing this version for publication, I have left the text of the original more or less untouched, apart from the addition of this preface, an index and some occasional footnotes discussing more recent literature.

The central argument of this work is that the syntax of finite subordinate clauses without *that* differs from corresponding clauses with an overt complementizer, such as the complement and relative clauses below:

> I said [it was true.]
> the chest [the key opened]

Evidence from embedded adjunction facts (adverbial adjunction and topicalization) is presented for the 'IP-hypothesis' of the structure of these clauses: i.e. that the bracketed constituents above are bare finite IPs, not CPs with a phonologically null head (the 'CP-hypothesis').

The outline of the work is as follows. Chapter 1 explores the theoretical background to the IP-hypothesis and its broader consequences. The empirical evidence for the proposal and its more specific empirical and theoretical consequences are then investigated in the following three major chapters of this work.

In Chapter 2, conceptual and empirical evidence for the IP-hypothesis of the structure of *that*-less argument clauses is presented and the question of their distribution addressed: one possible objection to the IP-hypothesis is that it is incompatible with the ECP account of the distribution of these clauses (Stowell 1981). It is argued, however, that the ECP account faces enough conceptual and empirical problems that its loss is not an objection to the IP-hypothesis. Finally, an appendix to this chapter explores the syntax of manner of speech verbs and noun complement clauses. A revised version of the main arguments of this chapter has appeared as Doherty 1997.

Chapter 3 presents evidence for the IP-hypothesis of *that*-less relatives (*contact clauses*). It is argued that the relative head directly A'-binds the gap in these constructions, without the apparatus of operator movement:

the chest$_i$ [$_{IP}$ the key opened e_i]

This proposal forms the basis for an explanation of the syntactic similarities and differences between contact and other 'full' relative clauses.

This chapter also contains an exploration of the syntax of 'subject contact clauses' which are common in (but not restricted to) Hiberno-English (i.e. tensed subject-gap relatives without an overt relative pronoun or complementizer):

There's someone ∅ wants to see you.

New evidence is provided that this is a true restrictive relative construction (*pace* McCawley 1981, 1988). This finding has quite broad consequences for theories of English relativization, as it then follows that no adequate approach can exclude subject contact clauses *a priori*.

In Chapter 4 the implications of the IP-hypothesis for A'-movement are explored, specifically for the *that*-trace effect. It is argued that the proposal allows for a maximal reduction of the complexity of previous accounts, in particular those based on the head-government relation (Rizzi 1990).

Chapter 5 concludes with a preview of the extension of the IP-hypothesis to the nonfinite domain.

Since 1993, some of the proposals made in this work have been adopted or further explored by other researchers. The IP-analysis of *that*-less complement clauses, in particular, has been adopted in constraint-based frameworks by Grimshaw 1997 and by Legendre, Smolensky and Wilson 1998. Working within the minimalist program, Bošković 1994 also adopts the IP-hypothesis, and in Bošković 1995 and 1997, extends it to non-finite clauses. This approach has also found its way into a recent textbook on the minimalist program, Radford (1997: 147-9).

Finally, further discussion of the phenomenon of subject contact clauses can be found in Henry 1995 (for Hiberno-English) and in Goodluck 1997, in which evidence from the acquisition of relative clauses is found to support the claim made here (and in Doherty 1993), that contact clauses lack successive-cyclic movement.

Acknowledgements

I owe a great debt of gratitude to my principal advisor, Jim McCloskey, and to the other members of my dissertation committee, Sandy Chung, Donka Farkas and Bill Ladusaw. Jim's work has been an inspiration to me over the years and I feel very fortunate to have had the benefit of his teaching and direction here in Santa Cruz as before in Dublin. I am grateful in particular for his time and encouragement while engaged in this project. Also, Bill, Donka and Sandy were all very generous with time and invaluable comments. I learned a great deal from our conversations both about this work and so many other things. I couldn't have hoped for a better dissertation committee.

I'm very glad I came to Santa Cruz. All the faculty not mentioned already, Judith Aissen, Jorge Hankamer, Junko Itô, Armin Mester and Geoff Pullum are inspiring teachers. I have learned much from each of them and thank them all.

I also want to thank fellow (ex-)students, other linguists and visitors to Santa Cruz for providing a lively environment in which to work: my classmates, Robin Schafer and Andy Black, also Giulia Centineo, Ted Fernald, Michele Hart, Marco Haverkort, Paula Iveland, Michael Johnston, Louise McNally, Peter Svenonius, Kari Swingle and Charles Wallace.

Thanks especially to Kari, Louise and Peter for much useful discussion about various aspects of this dissertation, to Kari and Peter for detailed comments on Chapter 2 and to Michael for some last-minute help with proof-reading.

Thanks also to my family and Siobhán Cottell for long-distance encouragement. This work was partially supported by a Humanities Predoctoral Fellowship from the University of California, Santa Cruz.

Clauses without "That"

CHAPTER 1

The Category of *That*-less Clauses

1. CLAUSE STRUCTURE

Although there has been agreement among syntacticians in recent years as to the optimal form of the phrase structure component, there have been widely-differing proposals as to the status of 'sentence' (S) within it. The consensus is that the phrase structure component should consist solely of general principles of well-formedness: i.e. principles of X'-theory (Chomsky 1970, Jackendoff 1977, Pullum 1985), rather than descriptive construction-specific or language-specific phrase structure rules, such as (1):

(1) S → NP Aux VP

All syntactic phrases are assumed to have a common structure, in which a head X^0 projects to a maximal projection X'' (or X''', as in Jackendoff 1977), with the optional presence of a specifier (Z'') or complement (Y''):

(2).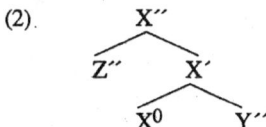

There are two main possibilities as to the status of the category sentence (S) within this program: (i) S does not conform to general principles of phrase structure at all. This is the position of Bresnan 1982 who claims that S is a non-maximal category which is not a projection of any element; (ii) S does conform to the general principles of phrase structure. This proposal is variously shared by Gazdar *et al.* 1985 and Jackendoff 1977 who take V^0 to be the head of S and by Chomsky 1986a who, extending the X´-schema to the minor category Infl(ection), proposes that S is the projection of Infl:

(3)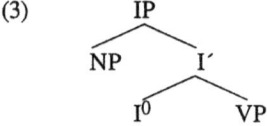

This proposal has been widely adopted in the 'principles and parameters' or 'government and binding' tradition.

In addition to the basic sentential category 'S', the need for the distinct clausal category 'S´´' has been recognized since Bresnan's work showing that complementizers are not transformationally inserted (Bresnan 1970, 1972, 1979). Specifically, presentential material such as *wh*-words and complementizers necessitate the following phrase structure rule, where COMP functions both as the locus for complementizers and the landing site for *wh*-movement.

(4) S´ → COMP S

Given that S´ appears in complement position, it is uncontroversial that it is a maximal projection. Bresnan 1982 proposes that S is the category from which S´ is projected. Chomsky 1986a, on the other hand, proposes that complementizers are the elements from which S´ is projected, i.e. that S´ is 'CP', a complementizer phrase:

(5)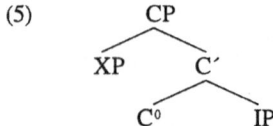

The proposals of Chomsky 1986a have been widely adopted and extended to a wide range of questions of clausal syntax, e.g. the clause structure of VSO languages (Chung 1990, McCloskey 1991).

2. A QUESTION

Although it is proposed that S is a maximal projection (IP), it never appears outside the complement of C^0, except (perhaps) as a root clause in declarative sentences:

(6) [$_{IP}$ John kissed Mary.]

However, given that the root clause is the largest syntactic phrase, it is impossible to determine with any degree of certainty what the category of the root really is. Although a root clause may be string-identical to IP (as in declaratives), the possibility always exists that the category of the root is something else. In fact, it is often assumed that all root sentences are S´ (CP) (e.g. Bresnan 1970: 301 n.4). Therefore, there is some degree of difficulty with the claim that S is a maximal projection (IP), in that it is not corroborated by the appearance of IP in complement or other non-root positions.

In most languages, finite subordinate clauses are always introduced by a complementizer and are therefore obviously of the category CP. However, English (and the Scandinavian languages) permits strings in complement positions which are identical to root declaratives, such as the bracketed material in (7):

(7) John says [this key opens the chest.]

The question is: what is the category of this bracketed constituent? Is it CP or IP? I refer to the latter position as the 'IP-hypothesis' and the former as the 'CP-hypothesis' throughout this work. If the IP-hypothesis is tenable, then, among other consequences, the status of IP as a maximal projection receives strong confirmation.

2.1. An Answer: the CP-hypothesis

Most previous work, however, assumes that subordinate clauses without overt complementizers are CP, the head of which has either been deleted or is base-generated as a null element (Chomsky and Lasnik 1977, Stowell 1981):[1]

(8) John said [$_{CP}$ ∅ [$_{IP}$ he kissed Mary.]]

The 'CP-hypothesis' of *that*-less complements has much to recommend it. First, from a cross-linguistic perspective, it regularizes the English situation. Secondly, the assumption that clausal complements are uniformly of the category CP avoids any potential complication of subcategorization frames.

However, the required free variation between null and overt C^0 raises some important questions. In particular, under the assumption that null complementizer are derived by deletion, a number of difficulties arise. First, a deletion process which targets solely (functional) heads is typologically strange in that attested deletion processes usually target phrasal material, not functional heads.[2] Assuming that such a deletion process is possible, it is somewhat surprising that other functional heads such as determiners do not undergo similar deletion rules.

(9)a. I read the book.
b. *I read book.

Secondly, assuming a theory in which the 'cheapest' among derivations with identical LF-interpretations blocks other competing derivations (e.g. Chomsky 1992), it must be the case that both *that*-clauses and clauses without *that* are equally valued. Otherwise, the free alternation between them in complement position would not be predicted. However, under the strictest interpretation of economy, in terms of the number of steps in a derivation, the transformational derivation of a *that*-less clause *via* deletion might be expected to be more 'expensive' than the corresponding *that*-clause.

Finally, under the assumption that null complementizers are lexically inserted, the free alternation between the null and overt form is unusual. Other null heads which have been posited for English (e.g. D^0) are either obligatorily null or obligatorily overt:

(10)a. [$_{DP}$ John's [$_{D'}$ Ø [$_{NP}$ book]]]

b. [$_{DP}$ Ø [$_{NP}$ Pigs]] fly badly.

c. *John's the book

d. The pigs fly badly. (wrong meaning)

Therefore, the proposed free alternation between CPs with null and overt heads is anomalous, in broader perspective.

I conclude therefore, that although the CP-hypothesis of the structure of *that*-less complement clauses has certain pleasing consequences, it incurs a certain cost. In particular, in order to correctly predict free alternation between *that*- and *that*-less clauses, appeal to a deletion rule or unprecedented free alternation between null and overt heads is required.

2.2. An Answer: the IP-hypothesis

This work provides novel evidence from adjunction facts that embedded *that*-less clauses are bare sentences of the category IP, rather than CP.[3] This argument is presented in detail in following chapters (for complement clauses in Chapter 2, and for relative clauses in Chapter 3).

I propose that the phenomenon of '*that*-deletion' in English complement clauses simply reflects the optional generation of bare finite IP in complement position:

(11)a. I said [IP John left.]

b. I said [CP that [IP John left.]]

That is, clauses without *that* are IP-complements and *that*-clauses are CP-complements.

The appearance of S (IP) in complement position, in addition to certain empirical predictions, has a some broad theoretical consequences. First, as pointed out previously, this result serves as confirmation for the status of S as a maximal projection in English, as proposed by Gazdar *et al.* 1985 and Chomsky 1986a.

Secondly, the IP-hypothesis has obvious implications for the theory of selection. In particular, it resonates with two strands of current research. It is compatible with the research program which seeks to eliminate c(ategory)-selection in favor of s(emantic-)selection (e.g. Pesetsky 1991). If IP and CP denote the same semantic entity (Proposition), then the free alternation between them as selected complements is predicted. Furthermore, it is compatible with the recent proposals by Grimshaw (Grimshaw 1991, 1993, 1997) that the clausal categories VP, IP and CP are categorially non-distinct and form an extended (verbal) projection. The alternation between IF and CP under this approach is then even compatible with a theory which demands (a form of) category selection.

In essence, the central proposal of this work is that subordinate finite clauses lacking a complementizer or other subordinating element are simply bare sentences (IP) which lack the CP-projection entirely. The three major chapters of this work investigate the more specific empirical and theoretical consequences of this claim in detail.

3. OUTLINE OF THE WORK

In Chapter 2, the distributional constraints on clauses without *that* are discussed. One apparent advantage of the CP-hypothesis of the structure of *that*-less clauses is that it yields an account of their exclusion from sentence-initial and other non-subcategorized positions:

(12)a. *(That) Clinton will be re-elected is unlikely.
  b. It bothers me *(that) it's so hot in October.

If null complementizers are subject to licensing by the Empty Category Principle (ECP), then these restrictions can be accounted for, as proposed in Stowell 1981. Under standard assumptions, non-subcategorized positions are not properly-governed.

However, this classical analysis suffers from conceptual and empirical problems. First, it is not clear why null complementizers should be subject to a proper government requirement in the first place. Secondly, there are empirical problems in that this analysis predicts that the set of clauses whose complementizers fulfill the requirements of the ECP is co-extensive with the set of clauses which permit grammatical *that*-deletion. This prediction is demonstrated to be false. There are complementizers which fulfill the structural requirements of proper government but which cannot be null. Furthermore, there are many instances of null complementizers in positions where they cannot be properly governed. Therefore, it is concluded that the incompatibility of the IP-hypothesis with this account is not a serious objection to the IP-hypothesis.

Chapter 3 discusses the phenomenon of relative clauses without *that* ('contact clauses' in terms of Jespersen 1909-49) and argues from adjunction facts that the category of the relative modifier is IP, rather than CP:

(13) the chest [$_{IP}$ the key opened e]

This presents somewhat of a paradox, in that under fairly standard assumptions, a clause must contain some syntactic correlate of λ-abstraction (i.e. an A´-chain) in order receive an interpretation as a relative clause, either overt *wh*-movement (as in the case of *wh*-relatives) or covert movement (as in the case of *that*-relatives). Furthermore, contact clauses display all the diagnostics of a syntactic A´-chain. However, I demonstrate that this structure is in fact compatible with current assumptions as to the structure and interpretation of relative clauses. Specifically, I propose that the relative head (the node to which the relative modifier is adjoined) is an A´-position which directly binds into the relativized position. Essentially, contact clauses are relative clauses which simply lack the apparatus of operator movement. Furthermore, the nature of the binding relation forms the basis for an account of the similarities and differences between contact relatives and other 'full' relative clauses. The contact clauses must be adjacent to the noun phrase they modify, as the integrity of the binding relation between the relative head and the gap must be maintained.

The final part of the chapter contains a detailed discussion of the phenomenon of 'subject contact clauses', which are grammatical only in what is loosely termed 'non-standard' speech and only in certain syntactic contexts, such as existentials:

(14) There's someone here wants to meet you.

Novel evidence is provided that the distribution of these clauses is wider than has been traditionally observed. Furthermore, I argue that the proposed analysis provides the basis for an understanding of the distributional constraints on this construction.

In Chapter 4, the implications of the IP-hypothesis for the explanation of the '*that*-trace' effect are explored: i.e. the relative ungrammaticality of subject extraction across overt complementizers:

(15) *Who$_i$ did Bill say that t_i left?

The IP-hypothesis reduces the analytical task involved in accounting for this effect considerably: in the absence of null complementizers in embedded declarative clauses, all that remains to be explained is the failure of subject extraction across overt complementizers. The consequences of IP-complementation for Rizzi's head-government account are examined in detail and it is demonstrated that the complexities of this account can be greatly reduced. In particular, in combination with the Vacuous Movement Hypothesis (George 1980, Chomsky 1986a) appeal to the stipulative mechanism of 'agreement in comp' can be completely abandoned.

Finally, Chapter 5 contains some closing remarks and briefly explores the extension of the IP-hypothesis to bare infinitive clauses, concluding that there are some preliminary indications in its favor.

NOTES

1. The notable exceptions are Grimshaw 1993 and Webelhuth 1992 who adopt the IP-hypothesis.
2. Gapping has been claimed to involve verb deletion, as proposed in Ross 1967:

    John bought the book and Mary _ the record.

    However, Hankamer 1979 provides reason to believe that the deleted constituent is not a verb but a variable, which sometimes, though not always, includes a verb.
3. Other work which adopts the IP-hypothesis for finite complement clauses includes Bowers 1987 and Webelhuth 1992, and since this dissertation first appeared, Bošković 1994, 1996, 1997 and Grimshaw 1997. The IP-hypothesis has also been proposed by Weisler 1980 for *that*-less relative clauses.

CHAPTER 2

Argument Clauses

1. INTRODUCTION

This chapter provides empirical evidence from adjunction facts that the IP-hypothesis of the structure of complement clauses without *that*, (1), is more appropriate than the CP hypothesis, (2):

(1) I said [IP you were right.]

(2) I said [CP Ø [IP you were right.]]

This evidence consists of the fact that there are significant differences in adjunction possibilities between *that*-clauses and *that*-less clauses which are unexpected under the CP-hypothesis but for which the IP-hypothesis provides a ready account. Therefore, it is proposed that in addition to the conceptual problems for the CP-hypothesis noted in the previous chapter, a strong case can be made for the IP-hypothesis on empirical grounds.

One possible remaining argument for the CP-hypothesis is that it provides the basis of a straightforward account of the restriction of *that*-less clauses to subcategorized complement positions. Note that complementizer-less clauses are not permitted in subject, topic or post-verbal non-subcategorized positions:

(3)a. *(That) Clinton will be re-elected is very likely.
   b. *(That) he would never do that again, Bill promised.
   c. It bothers me *(that) it's so hot in October.

If it is assumed, following Stowell 1981 (citing earlier work by Kayne), that null complementizers are subject to the Empty Category Principle (ECP) (Chomsky 1981, Stowell 1981), then the major distributional restrictions are accounted for: only subcategorized complement positions are properly governed under standard conceptions of the ECP.

In this chapter, I demonstrate that this classical analysis is problematic enough on both a conceptual and empirical level so as to warrant a reconsideration of its success; on a conceptual level because it is not clear why null complementizers should require proper government in the first place and on an empirical level because the analysis incorrectly predicts that the set of clauses whose complementizers meet the proper government requirement should be coextensive with the set of clauses which allow *that* to be absent. It is shown that this prediction is false: the correspondence between '*that*-deletion' and proper government is not exact. In particular, there are instances of complementizers which fulfill the structural requirements of proper government and yet cannot be null (e.g. in embedded sentential subjects). Likewise, null complementizers appear in positions which are neither subcategorized nor properly governed (e.g. in relative clauses). Given these problems, I conclude that incompatibility with the ECP account is not an argument against the IP-hypothesis.

The structure of the chapter is as follows: in section 2, the evidence in favor of the IP-hypothesis is presented in detail. In section 3, the classical ECP analysis of the distribution of *that*-less clauses is outlined and its difficulties explored. Section 4 examines the question of the distribution of *that*-less clauses under the IP-hypothesis. Finally, an appendix, section 6, treats the lexical restrictions on '*that*-deletion,' i.e. the fact that certain lexical items (e.g. manner of speech verbs) do not permit *that*-less complements.

2. ARGUMENTS FOR THE IP-HYPOTHESIS

If *that*-less clauses have exactly the structure of *that*-clauses, as the CP-hypothesis maintains, then it would be expected that both clause-types display the same syntactic characteristics. However, this is not the case: there are significant differences with respect to adjunction possibilities. In the following discussion, I show that it is not obvious how these facts can be accounted for under the CP-hypothesis and demonstrate that the IP-hypothesis makes available a straightforward account of the data.

2.1. Embedded Topicalization

Note that embedded Topics must appear internal to the complement clause, to the right of the complementizer.

(4)a. I hope that *this book* you will read.
   b. She claims that *Guinness* he likes but that whiskey he hates.
   c. This proves that *Cinque* he'd read but that Rizzi he hadn't.

They cannot appear to the left of the complementizer:

(5)a. *I hope *this book* that you will read.
   b. *She claims *Guinness* that he likes but that whiskey he hates.
   c. *This proves *Cinque* that he'd read but that Rizzi he hadn't.

This observation provides the basis of an argument for the IP-hypothesis. There are two major approaches to Topicalization: (i) movement to a phrase intermediate between CP and IP (Authier 1992; Chomsky 1977; Culicover 1991; Müller and Sternefeld 1994);[1] (ii) as adjunction to IP (Lasnik and Saito 1992; Rochemont 1989):

(6)a. [$_{CP}$ that [$_{TopicP}$ *Topic* [$_{IP}$ ...]]]

   b. [$_{CP}$ that [$_{IP}$ *Topic* [$_{IP}$ ...]]]

Assuming the CP-hypothesis, both analyses predict that Topicalization in embedded clauses without *that* is possible. As illustrated schematically in (7), whether the complementizer is overt or null has no obvious bearing on the possibility of Topicalization:

(7)a. [$_{CP}$ Ø [$_{TopicP}$ *Topic* [$_{IP}$ ...]]]

   b. [$_{CP}$ Ø [$_{IP}$ *Topic* [$_{IP}$ ...]]]

However, this prediction is incorrect: embedded Topicalization in *that*-less clauses is robustly ungrammatical:

(8)a. *I hope *this book* you will read.
   b. *She claims *Guinness* he likes but whiskey he hates.
   c. *This proves *Cinque* he'd read but Rizzi he hadn't.

There is no obvious explanation for these facts under the CP-hypothesis.

However, a ready explanation is available under the IP-hypothesis. First, under the assumption that Topicalization is movement to a phrase intermediate between IP and CP, there is simply no available landing site. Second, under the adjunction to IP analysis an account is also available: if the failure of adjunction to complement CP, as in (5) above, shows that adjunction to the outside of a complement clause is excluded in principle, then adjunction to an IP complement is also excluded by the same principle.

It is an interesting question as to what this principle is, however. The Adjunction Prohibition (McCloskey 1992: 11) is a plausible candidate.[2]

(9) *Adjunction Prohibition*

Adjunction to a phrase which is s-selected by a lexical head is ungrammatical.

This principle is consistent with the fact that embedded Topicalization (interpreted as adjunction to IP) is permitted to the right of the complementizer *that*:

(10)a. I hope [$_{CP}$ that [$_{IP}$ *this book* [$_{IP}$ you will read.]]]

b. She claims [$_{CP}$ that [$_{IP}$ *Guinness* [$_{IP}$ he likes but whiskey he hates.]]]

c. This proves [$_{CP}$ that [$_{IP}$ *Cinque* [$_{IP}$ I'd read but Rizzi I hadn't..]]]

As the IP complement of C^0 is not selected by a lexical head, nothing prevents adjunction to IP. However, adjunction to the CP level (to the left of the complementizer) is correctly predicted to be ungrammatical, as the CP is directly s-selected by the matrix verb:

(11)a. *I hope [$_{CP}$ *this book* [$_{CP}$ that you will read.]]

b. *She claims [$_{CP}$ *Guinness* [$_{CP}$ that he likes but whiskey he hates.]]

c. *This proves [$_{CP}$ *Cinque* [$_{CP}$ that he'd read but Rizzi he hadn't.]]

Similarly, the Adjunction Prohibition rules out adjunction to complement IP:

(12)a. *I think [IP *this book* [IP you should read.]]

b. *He said [IP *beer* [IP he likes but whiskey he hates.]]

c. *He says [IP *Cinque* [IP he'd read but Rizzi he hadn't.]]

Therefore, I conclude that there is positive evidence in favor of the IP-hypothesis. Unlike the CP-hypothesis, it provides the basis for an explanation of the failure of embedded Topicalization in *that*-less complements.

2.2. Adverbial Adjunction

In the general case, adverbial adjunction follows the same pattern as Topicalization: sentential adverbs must appear to the right of the complementizer, presumably adjoined to the IP-level.

(13)a. She prayed that *next Wednesday* the check would arrive.
b. We concluded that *in the future* he should be closely watched.
c. We maintain that *in Dublin* good coffee is hard to find.
d. John claims that *during the party* Ted squirted water at Eric.

Adjunction to the CP-level is excluded (on an embedded construal):

(14)a. *She prayed *next Wednesday* that the check would arrive.
b. *We concluded *in the future* that he should be closely watched.
c. *We maintain *in Dublin* that good coffee is hard to find.
d. *John claims *during the party* that Ted squirted water at Eric.

This observation provides the basis of another argument for the IP-hypothesis.

Under the CP-hypothesis, it would be expected (all things being equal) that adverbial adjunction to a *that*-less clause should be grammatical on a par with adjunction to a *that*-clause. As illustrated schematically below, adjunction to IP to the right of a null complementizer is expected to be as grammatical as adjunction to IP to the right of an overt complementizer:

(15) a. V^0 [$_{CP}$ ∅ [$_{IP}$ *Adverb* [$_{IP}$ ...]]]

b. V^0 [$_{CP}$ that [$_{IP}$ *Adverb* [$_{IP}$ ...]]]

However, this prediction is not borne out. The sentences in (14) above seem robustly ungrammatical without *that*:

(16) a. *She prayed *next Wednesday* the check would arrive.
b. *We concluded *in the future* he should be closely watched.
c. *We maintain *in Dublin* good coffee is hard to find.
d. *John claims *during the party* Ted squirted water at Eric.

There is no obvious account for this fact under the CP-hypothesis.

However, the IP-hypothesis provides a solution: if adverbial adjunction to the maximal projection of a complement clause is excluded by some principle, as suggested by the ungrammaticality of adjunction to CP in (14) above, then adjunction to the maximal projection of an IP-complement should also be ungrammatical. As discussed in the previous section, a plausible candidate for this principle is the Adjunction Prohibition.

There are some apparent counterexamples to this argument in that adverbial adjunction to *that*-less complements seems, in many cases, to be fully grammatical:

(17) a. She says (that) *when we get home* things will be different.
b. I believe (that) *next year* she'll be fine.
c. I suppose (that) *ordinarily* you would go somewhere else.
d. He thinks (that) *in some circumstances* things would be better.

However, these examples do not constitute counterexamples to the IP-hypothesis, I argue. This is because in all these cases, the adverb can appear to the left of the complementizer with no significant change in acceptability:

(18) a. She says *when we get home* that things will be different.
b. I believe *next year* that she'll be fine.
c. I suppose *ordinarily* that you would go somewhere else.
d. He thinks *in some circumstances* that things would be better.

If the adverb can apparently adjoin to a CP complement, then there is no reason not to expect it to adjoin to an IP complement. Rather than constituting counterexamples to the IP-hypothesis, these examples are problematic for the form of the Adjunction Prohibition in (9) above.

It is an interesting question (though one tangential to the main point here) what is responsible for these facts. There are a couple of relevant observations. First, the verbs in examples like (17) and (18) are typically those which permit a parenthetical use:

(19)a. He'll be here next week, I (believe/think/suppose ...)
 b. He'll be here, I (believe/think/suppose ...) next week.

Therefore, it seems possible that the instances of these verbs in (17) are, in fact, parentheticals. Now, a mark of parentheticals is their incompatibility with negation. Interestingly, the examples in (17) and (18) are quite ungrammatical with matrix negation:

(20)a. *She doesn't say when we get home (that) things will be different.
 b. *I don't believe next year (that) she'll be fine.
 c. *I don't think ordinarily (that) you would go someplace else.
 d. *He doesn't think in some circumstances (that) things would be better.

Therefore, it seems plausible that the apparent violations of the Adjunction Prohibition in (17) follow from the fact that the 'matrix' verb is a parenthetical and the 'complement' clause is in fact a matrix clause, accounting for the possibility of adverbial adjunction.

The second observation is that, in many of these examples, the adverb is compatible with both a matrix and a complement construal. Therefore, the apparent ability of the adverb to 'flip over' the complementizer, as in (18), may be due to a garden path. However, if this were the entire explanation, each instance of an adverb which appears to the left of *that* should receive a matrix construal. This is not immediately obvious in the case of (18)a and (18)b, however.[3]

2.3. Adjunction Evidence: Summary

In sum, the CP-hypothesis, which maintains that both *that* and *that*-less clauses have identical syntactic structures, makes incorrect predictions with respect to embedded adjunction. First, it predicts that Topicalization should be possible in *that*-less clauses, a prediction which was shown to be false. Second, it predicts that adverbial adjunction to the left-edge of a *that*-less clause should always be possible. This prediction was also shown to be false. However, in both cases, the IP-hypothesis provides a ready answer for the facts. I conclude, therefore, that there is some positive evidence which tells in favor of the IP-hypothesis over the CP-hypothesis of the structure of *that*-less complement clauses.

3. THE ECP ACCOUNT OF THE DISTRIBUTION OF *THAT*-LESS CLAUSES

One possible argument in favor of the CP-hypothesis of *that*-less clauses is that it provides the basis of an explanation of their restricted syntactic distribution: if it is assumed that null complementizers, like the traces of movement, are subject to licensing by the ECP, then the major distributional patterns can be accounted for (Stowell 1981).

The definition of the ECP has undergone much revision since Stowell 1981:[4] recent work (Rizzi 1990, Chomsky and Lasnik 1991) adopts the 'conjunctive ECP', which comprises two components: 'formal licensing' in the form of proper head-government and 'identification' in the form of antecedent government (Rizzi 1990: 32):

(21) *Empty Category Principle*

A non-pronominal empty category must be

(i) properly head-governed (formal licensing)
(ii) antecedent governed or Theta-governed (identification)

It is generally agreed that only head-government is relevant to the proper government of null complementizers (Aoun *et al.* 1987, Pesetsky 1991). As no syntactic movement is involved in the generation of null complementizers, antecedent government is irrelevant.[5] The requirement of proper head-government on null complementizers straightforwardly accounts for the major distributional patterns of *that*-less clauses. In the system of Rizzi 1990, proper head-government is defined as head-government under c-command:[6]

(22) *Proper Head Government*

α properly head-governs β, if α head-governs β and α c-commands β.

Head-government is defined as follows (Rizzi 1990: 6):[7]

(23)   *Head Government:*

X head-governs Y iff.

(i)   X ∈ {A, N, P, V, Agr, T}
(ii) X m-commands Y
(iii) no barrier intervenes
(iv) Relativized Minimality is respected.

These definitions ensure that complementizers in complement clauses are properly head-governed by the matrix verb:

(24) I said [$_{CP}$ [$_{C'}$ [$_{CP}$ Ø] [$_{IP}$ you were right.]]]

The m-command relation holds; the complement clause is subcategorized by the matrix verb and therefore lexically (L-) marked by it, ensuring that it is not a barrier. Furthermore, no other possible head-governor intervenes between them, i.e. Relativized Minimality is respected (Rizzi 1990: 7):

(25)   *Relativized Minimality*:

X α-governs Y if and only if there is no Z such that:

(i) Z is a potential α-governor for Y,
(ii) Z c-commands Y and does not c-command X.

There is no potential governor intervening between the matrix V^0 and the embedded C^0 to count as Z in the above definition. Therefore, the licensing of null complementizers in complement clauses follows.

On the other hand, clauses in non-complement positions are not in a configuration for proper head-government: sentence-initial clauses lack a potential head-governor entirely. Furthermore, adjunct and extraposed clauses are not in a position where they can be properly head-governed from V^0 or I^0. Furthermore, as these clauses are barriers to government (they are in non-L-marked positions), government from external heads is excluded. Therefore, the failure of null complementizers in these environments is straightforwardly predicted and the empirical coverage of the head-government account appears to be considerable.

3.1. The Government Requirement

However, it is not clear why null complementizers should be subject to the ECP at all. If the ECP is a unitary principle requiring both antecedent and head-government, then why should null complementizers, which do not involve syntactic movement, be subject to the ECP? By definition, they cannot satisfy antecedent government. The claim that null C^0 requires head-government also entails that unless there is strong reason to suggest the contrary, it is expected that other null syntactic heads are subject to the same licensing requirement. However, this is clearly not the case: other null heads which have been proposed for English cannot be constrained by a requirement of proper head-government. In particular, null determiners have no distributional restrictions and appear freely in subject position.[8]

(26) [DP John's [D' ∅ [NP hat]]] fell.

Furthermore, there are complementizers which cannot be head-governed in terms of the above definitions which can, and in fact must, be null:

(27) the man [CP who [C' ∅ [IP John met *t*]]]

This fact necessitates a complication of the theory to exclude these null complementizers from ECP requirements, which is discussed in more detail in 3.3 below.

3.2. Explaining the Government Requirement

Some recent work attempts to raise the claim that null complementizers are subject to a proper head-government requirement above the level of a stipulation. Proposals include Pesetsky 1991 who claims that null complementizers are derived through syntactic movement and Hornstein and Lightfoot 1992 who claim that all null elements are subject to the same government requirement. I briefly consider these two approaches below.

3.2.1. C^0 to V^0 Incorporation

In recent unpublished work Pesetsky (1991: 39-46) has proposed an account of '*that*-deletion' in terms of head-movement. Specifically, he proposes that null complementizers are base-generated and must raise to the matrix V^0 in the syntax, due to their morphological characteristics, as indicated schematically below:[9]

(28)

```
        V⁰      CP
                 \
                  C'
                 / \
                C⁰  IP
                |
                ∅
```

This proposal has the pleasing consequence of providing a solid theoretical foundation for the claim that null complementizers must be properly head-governed: under standard conceptions, the trace of head-movement is subject to the ECP. However, aside from the fact that overt C^0 to V^0 incorporation is not attested in any language (a problem pointed out by Pesetsky[10]) this account makes some incorrect predictions regarding the co-ordination of complement CPs. In particular, if head-movement is constrained by the Co-ordinate Structure Constraint (CSC), it would be unexpected that C^0 to V^0 movement could proceed out of conjoined complement clauses. This makes some interesting predictions as to the co-ordination possibilities of *that* and *that*-less clauses.

All the evidence suggests that head-movement in English is subject to the CSC. Consider the case of co-ordinated auxiliaries, such as in (29) below (I assume co-ordination of I^0 in these cases):

(29)
```
              IP
             /  \
           DP    I'
          John  / \
               I⁰  VP
              /|\   \
             I⁰ and I⁰  go home
             |      |
            can   should
```

If head-movement obeys the CSC, it would be expected that I^0 to C^0 movement should be excluded from such structures, as they would necessarily induce a CSC violation. This appears to be borne out:[11]

(30) *[$_{CP}$ What [$_{C'}$ can$_i$ [$_{IP}$ John [$_{I^0}$ t_i and should] do?]]]

Furthermore, note that I^0 to C^0 movement from co-ordinate IPs is ungrammatical:

(31) *What can$_i$ [$_{IP}$ John t$_i$ eat] and [$_{IP}$ Mary should not eat?]

Extraction from one conjunct of a co-ordinated I´ structure is also ungrammatical:

(32) *Which book should$_i$ [$_{IP}$ we [[$_{I'}$ t$_i$ read next] and [$_{I'}$ might enjoy]]]?

However, in both cases, movement originating in both conjuncts ('Across the Board' movement in the sense of Williams 1978) is grammatical:[12]

(33) What can$_i$ [$_{IP}$ John t$_i$ eat] and [Mary t$_i$ not eat?]

(34) Which book should$_i$ [$_{IP}$ we [$_{I'}$ [t$_i$ read next] and [$_{I'}$ t$_i$ try to enjoy?]]]

Given this conclusion, it would be expected that C^0 to V^0 movement is ungrammatical when movement originates in only one conjunct of a co-ordinate CP complement, as illustrated schematically in (35)a. However, it would be expected that movement originating in both conjuncts should be grammatical, as illustrated in (35)b.

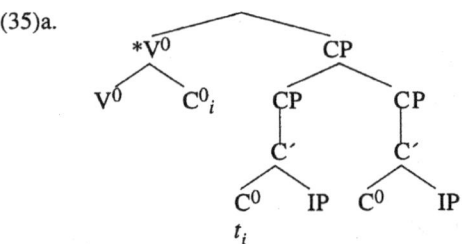

This makes two predictions: (i) a *that*-clause should not co-ordinate with a *that*-less clause, as such a structure could only be generated through a violation of the CSC, as in (35)a; (ii) co-ordination of two *that*-less clauses should be possible, by the 'Across the Board' derivation in (35)b. The latter prediction seems to be borne out:

(36) I believe [you are right] and [he is wrong.]

However, the former is not: *that*-clauses seem to freely conjoin with *that*-less clauses as in the following examples:[13]

(37)a. I believe [that he's right] and [you're wrong.]
   b. I hope [that you can come] and [Harry can too.]
   c. I think [that he'll come] and [he'll bring some friends.]

These examples are open to an alternative analysis as IPs co-ordinate under the one complementizer. Such an analysis is unavailable, however, when the rightmost conjunct is a *that*-clause:

(38)a. I believe [he is right] and [that you are wrong].
   b. I hope [you can come] and [that Harry can too].
   c. I think [he'll arrive on time] and [that he'll bring some friends also].

These examples are fully grammatical, however. Therefore, if they are truly examples of the co-ordination of subordinate *that* and *that*-less clauses, they are recalcitrant for Pesetsky's analysis in that they can only be derived through a violation of the CSC, yet there is every indication that head-movement in English is constrained by the CSC.

However, some more work is required to make the point. There is some possibility that these co-ordinate structures are open to an analysis as co-ordinate matrix sentences, where ellipsis in the second conjunct removes the predicate under identity, stranding the complement clause:

(39) [I believe that he is right] and [∅ you are wrong.]

However, we can eliminate this possibility. Consider the following example where the matrix negation licenses a negative polarity item in the right conjunct:

(40) I don't believe [he is lying] or [that anyone else is *either.*]

The licensing of the polarity item indicates clearly that the clause is c-commanded by, and therefore subordinate to, the matrix negation. Therefore, it seems that this example must instantiate the co-ordination of a *that* and a *that*-less complement, which as discussed above, is recalcitrant for Pesetsky's approach.

3.2.2. Head Government at Phonological Form

Hornstein and Lightfoot 1992 and earlier work by Aoun, Hornstein, Lightfoot and Weinberg 1987 propose that null elements require government by a lexical head (lexical government) at the level of Phonological Form (PF). Evidence for this claim is provided from processes such as Gapping and preposition stranding. I refer the reader to the relevant works: what is of central concern to this discussion is not whether a PF government constraint on null elements is motivated but whether this proposal is sufficient to account for the specific syntactic restrictions on *that*-deletion. I conclude below that it is not.

Hornstein and Lightfoot (1992: 368-9) argue that the supposed non-availability of *that*-deletion in clauses which have undergone Right Node Raising (RNR), illustrated in (41) below, provides a strong argument that the constraints on *that*-deletion apply at PF and not at s-structure.

(41) Fay believes and Kay asserted publicly *(that) John lied.

They assume that RNR is a post-syntactic rule, as it does not affect binding relations, which they assume to hold of s-structure. The fact that they are unaffected by RNR indicates that this rule applies at a level later than s-structure. For example, note that *him* must be interpreted as disjoint from both *John* and *Jim* in the following example of RNR:

(42) *Jim* wants and *John* expects *him* to win.

It would be expected that coreference with *Jim* would be allowed if RNR and the binding conditions applied at the same level. Therefore, they claim:

"Whether the binding theory holds at S-Structure or at LF, then, there needs to be a condition of lexical government that determines the deletability of complementizers and applies to a level of representation after S-Structure and after RNR has applied - namely, at PF. This is not to say of course that the condition holds of a purely phonetic representation, but rather at some appropriate level of abstraction on the PF side of the grammar on the basis of which phonetic representation is determined." (*op. cit.*, 369)

However, this argument seems tenuous. First, it is not clear that RNR fails to target *that*-less clauses (Kari Swingle p.c.). Consider the following examples which are fully grammatical for many speakers.

(43) a. I really think but Mary doubts Clinton will be elected.
   b. The Serbs think and the Muslims openly claim he is dishonest.
   c. The Unionists fear but most Nationalists fervently hope the Anglo-Irish agreement will remain intact after the talks.

Secondly, even if RNR did not target *that*-less clauses, it does not necessarily follow that the relevant constraint on '*that*-deletion' is located at PF. This argument rests on the assumption that both *that*-clauses and *that*-less clauses are syntactically the same entity, i.e. CP. However, if *that*-less clauses are categorially distinct from *that*-clauses (the former IP, the latter CP) then the argument loses force: RNR may simply target CP and not IP.[14]

A more serious problem for this PF-based approach is the fact that string-adjacency is not required for grammatical *that*-deletion. Hornstein and Lightfoot (1992: 387 n.3) point out that the presence of an adverb between the matrix verb and the complement clause excludes the possibility of *that*-deletion:

(44) I believe sincerely *(that) Kay will be elected.

They claim that lexical government requires adjacency and that the failure of adjacency in this example is responsible for the ungrammaticality. However, this claim is not obviously reconcilable with the fact that many other adverbs do not induce a comparable effect:

(45) a. I think in general people tend to like him.
   b. They said last year the economy would be better by now.
   c. I used to think back then she'd never make it at all.
   d. I believe myself she is a good person.

Furthermore, argument phrases can freely intervene between a (subcategorized) *that*-less clause and the matrix predicate, as in (46):

(46) a. It seems to me (that) he's on the right track.
   b. I said to Mary (that) he was in error.

However, if an adjunct phrase intervenes, *that*-deletion is ungrammatical:

(47) It was believed by everyone *(that) he was on the right track.

In these cases, the complement clause is presumably extraposed to a sentence-final adjunct position. Therefore, it is clear that the acceptability of *that*-deletion cannot simply rely on string-adjacency. The relevant constraint must have access to enough syntactic structure to distinguish between argument complements and adjuncts. However, this appeal to syntactic information undermines the claim that the relevant constraint on *that*-deletion is located at PF. This becomes especially apparent when we consider the case of manner of speech verbs:

(48)a. Fay quipped *(that) Kay left.
  b. Fay said (that) Kay left.

Adjacency is obviously irrelevant here. Aoun *et al.* 1987 propose that these verbs are defective governors (citing previous work by Aoun 1985, Kayne 1981a,b and Stowell 1981): i.e. they can properly govern a direct object, as in (49) below, but they cannot properly govern into the 'Comp' of the complement clause, accounting for the failure of *that*-deletion.[15]

(49) What$_i$ did Fay whisper t_i ?

However, whatever the ultimate analysis of these facts, it seems clear that access to significant syntactic information is required to account for the failure of *that*-deletion in these constructions. Again this serves to undermine the claim that the constraint on *that*-deletion is located at PF.

In conclusion, Aoun *et al.* 1987 and Hornstein and Lightfoot 1992 claim that the licensing of null elements is constrained by a lexical government requirement at PF. They propose that the distribution of *that*-deletion (interpreted as licensing requirements on null complementizers) is accounted for by this PF constraint. Assuming that their claim that all null elements require PF-government is tenable (a claim which faces some difficulties given the discussion in 3.1), then the statement that null complementizers are subject to a government requirement is raised from the level of stipulation, if they too fall under this PF-government constraint. However, there are two problems: (i) as just discussed, there is no evidence that the government constraint on null complementizers lies in PF as opposed to syntax; (ii) as discussed

Argument Clauses

in the following section, there are many instances of null elements (complementizers and other heads) which are apparently exempt from any government requirements at all, whether at PF or surface syntax.

3.2.3. Conclusion

In conclusion, the central assumption of ECP-based approaches to the distribution of *that*-less clauses is that null complementizers require proper government, like the traces of moved elements or other null material. This assumption, however, has the status of a stipulation unless (i) null complementizers really are the trace of syntactic movement (Pesetsky 1991); or, (ii) they are subject to the same PF-government constraint as other null material (Hornstein and Lightfoot 1992). However, as discussed in the previous sections, neither of these alternatives seem tenable. Therefore, I conclude that the proper government requirement on null C^0 remains at the level of a stipulation.

3.3. Empirical Problems

The classical ECP analysis crucially hinges on the claim that the sole licensing factor for *that*-deletion is proper government (head-government or lexical government at PF). Therefore, the set of clauses whose complementizer-heads meet the proper head-government requirement and the set of clauses which admit grammatical *that*-deletion should be co-extensive. In the general case, this appears to be true, as outlined in the introduction. However, on closer inspection some cracks appear: (i) there are instances of clauses whose complementizers clearly fulfill the structural requirements for proper head-government but which reject *that*-deletion; (ii) there are also instances of null complementizers which cannot be properly head-governed under standard definitions.

3.3.1. Embedded Sentential Subjects

Embedded sentential subjects, such as in (50) below, are marginal at best for many speakers.[16] However, there is a clear contrast in acceptability between the form with *that*-deletion and the form without:

(50) I believe [[$_{CP}$ *(that) the end is nigh] to be obvious.]

This contrast is unexpected if the complementizer of the sentential subject is properly governed. First, assuming that the relevant licensing condition on *that*-deletion is lexical government at PF, following Hornstein and Lightfoot, it is not clear how this complementizer escapes lexical government, as it is string-adjacent to a verb. Second, assuming that the relevant licensing condition is syntactic proper head-government, it is also unclear why the complementizer must be overt, as all the structural requirements of head-government are met, as discussed below.

Chomsky (1986a: 25-26) argues that selecting heads L-mark into the specifiers of their complements. This accounts for the relative grammaticality of extraction from the specifier of CP and from the subject of ECM and small clause complements:

(51)a. This is the author by whom$_i$ we don't know [$_{CP}$ what books t_i [$_{IP}$ to read.]]
   b. Who$_i$ do you believe [$_{IP}$ [friends of t_i] to be stupid?]]
   c. Who$_i$ do you consider [$_{SC}$ [friends of t_i] stupid?]]

The matrix verb L-marks the specifier of its complement in each case, it is claimed. Therefore, the phrase in the specifier position does not constitute a barrier to extraction and the grammaticality of examples such as the above is predicted.

Adopting the common assumption that ECM verbs take nonfinite IP complements (Bresnan 1972, 1979; Chomsky 1981) it would be expected that the specifier position (the subject) of the IP-complement is L-marked by the matrix verb.[17] As the IP-complement is itself subcategorized and L-marked, the specifier of IP should also be L-marked, following Chomsky 1986a. This is borne out by the grammaticality of extraction from the subject position:

(52) This is the politician that I consider [supporters of _] to be fascists.

This conclusion suggests strongly that the complementizer position of sentential subjects in ECM complements, as in (53) below, is properly head-governed:

(53) I consider [$_{IP}$ [*(that) he is an idiot] to be obvious].

The m-command relation holds between the matrix verb and the complementizer and as IP is L-marked, no barrier intervenes between them. Also, as no governor intervenes, Relativized Minimality is respected. Therefore, all the indications are that the complementizer of the embedded clause is properly head-governed, which fails to account for the severe degradation associated with '*that*-deletion' in these contexts.

The argument is complicated somewhat by the fact that embedded sentential subjects reject extraction:

(54) *What do you consider [IP [that Mary will do *t*] to be obvious?]

However, the islandhood of these clauses cannot be due to a failure of L-marking, given the grammaticality of the corresponding extractions from nominals: all the structural requirements for L-marking from the matrix are met and the corresponding nominals are clearly L-marked. The islandhood of the embedded sentential subject must be due to some independent factor.[18] Therefore, there is a difficulty for the classical account here in that the structural requirements for government of the complementizer are met, and yet a null variant is not permitted.

A similar point is raised by the sentential complements of prepositional elements such as *before*, *after* and *since*. These constructions have received two major analyses in the recent literature: (i) as prepositions taking IP complements (McCloskey 1992, Webelhuth 1992); (ii) as simple complementizers (Dubinsky and Williams 1995; Huang 1982, Lasnik and Saito 1992), as respectively illustrated below:

(55)a. [PP [P0 after] [IP we got home]]
  b. [CP [C0 after] [IP we got home]]

It seems reasonable that the prepositional element selects and therefore L-marks its (IP) complement under either analysis. As pointed out by Lasnik and Saito (1992: 91), extraction from these clauses is not as ungrammatical as would be expected if the prepositional element did not select its clausal complement.[19]

(56) ??Which linguist did you write your thesis after you consulted *t* ?

They point out that examples such as the above have the flavor of simple adjunct island violations. If the clausal complement of the preposition were not subcategorized, the degree of ungrammaticality would be expected to be much greater. In addition, McCloskey (1992: 11) shows that in common with other selected phrases, the complements of these prepositional elements reject adjunction. This is illustrated by the following examples of embedded Topicalization:

(57) a. *I haven't seen her since Dublin I went to *t*.
b. *Before that rubbish people began to accept *t*, we were happier.
c. *After that kind of nonsense the professor heard *t*, he exploded.

The failure of adjunction is consistent with a selectional relationship between the prepositional element and the clause. Therefore, there is a reasonable body of evidence indicating that these prepositional heads select and L-mark their IP complements. Following Chomksy 1986a, the specifier of that IP is also L-marked. Therefore, it is expected that proper head-government holds between the prepositional head and the complementizer of an embedded sentential subject: the m-command relation holds, no barrier intervenes and Relativized Minimality is respected. However, this fails to predict the severe degradation associated with *that*-deletion in these clauses:

(58) a. Before *(that) Perot would re-enter the campaign became known, people in general favored Bush.

b. After *(that) Bush had lost California became known the Clinton camp rejoiced.

Although sentential subjects in this environment are marginal, the deletion of *that* clearly induces a more severe level of ungrammaticality. Unfortunately, it is difficult to corroborate the presence of L-marking with extraction facts. As these clauses are adjunct islands in themselves, it is difficult to decide whether subject extraction from a nominal is of the same status as complement extraction:[20]

(59) a. *?Which politician$_i$ did you meet before [the press discredited t_i]?
b. *?Which politician$_i$ did you meet before [that the press had discredited t_i became clear]?

In sum, there is a difficulty for the claim that proper government determines the distribution of *that*-deletion (null complementizers) in that embedded sentential subjects fulfill the structural requirements for head-government and yet do not permit *that*-deletion. The argument is admittedly complicated somewhat by the failure of extraction from these clauses. These facts are also recalcitrant for the proposal of Aoun *et al.* 1987 and Hornstein and Lightfoot 1992 that lexical government at PF determines the distribution of null complementizers: assuming lexical government holds under adjacency, the complementizer of an embedded sentential subject is lexically governed by the matrix verb.

3.3.2. Ungoverned Null Complementizers

Another difficulty for the classical ECP analysis is that a statement such as (60) below is simply inaccurate for English:

(60) [$_{C^0}$ ∅] must be properly governed.

The problem is that there are instances of grammatical zero complementizers in positions which are not properly governed. I consider three major cases below: (i) local subject extraction; (ii) relative clauses; (iii) degree clauses.

Under the assumption that local subject extraction involves movement to CP, then matrix interrogative CPs and *wh*-relatives instantiate null complementizers which cannot be head-governed under the usual definitions.[21]

(61)a. [$_{CP}$ Who$_i$ [$_{C'}$ ∅ [$_{IP}$ t_i left]]]?

   b. the man [$_{CP}$ who$_i$ [$_{C'}$ ∅ [t_i left]]]

These complementizers cannot be properly governed under the definitions of Rizzi 1990. In the case of matrix interrogatives, there is no potential proper governor for the complementizer at all. In the case of relative clauses, there is also no proper governor for C^0, as relative clauses are barriers to government from without, being non-θ-marked, non-L-marked adjuncts.

How can a distinction be drawn between these complementizers and those in complement clauses?[22] One possible line of analysis is to assume that null complementizers in complement clauses are derived through a syntactic deletion process, the output of which is subject to the ECP (or visible at PF in Hornstein and Lightfoot's terms). Local subject *wh*-extraction, on the other hand, involves base-generation of null complementizers, which for some reason are not subject to a government requirement. However, this distinction necessitates a significant complication of the theory in that it requires two distinct null complementizers with differing government requirements.

Relative clauses provide another instance of the problem. Consider the case of object-gap *wh*-relatives:

(62) the man [$_{CP}$ who$_i$ [$_{C'}$ ∅ [$_{IP}$ Mary likes t_i]]]

Assuming that relative operators move to the specifier of CP, there must be a morphologically null complementizer present in this structure. However, a null complementizer in this construction cannot be properly governed, as (i) under the standard adjunction analysis of relative clauses, there is no potential head-governor and (ii) relative clauses are barriers to government, as they are not θ-marked, L-marked phrases.[23]

The grammaticality of *that*-deletion in 'degree clauses' (Jackendoff 1977, Rothstein 1991), as illustrated below, also poses a problem for the classical ECP approach to the distribution of *that*-less complements.

(63)a. I ate so much food (that) I thought I'd be sick.
   b. It was so hot (that) the tar melted.

The syntax of this construction is not well-understood. However, given that specifiers in English appear exclusively on the left, it must be the case that the degree clause is a syntactic adjunct. There seem to be two main structural possibilities: (i) the degree clause is base-generated in its surface position, in which case the syntax of the construction resembles that of relative clauses and the degree clause is some kind of modifier; (ii) the degree clause is a D-structure complement of the degree word and is extraposed by s-structure. Both general approaches have been suggested in the literature and are discussed at length in Jackendoff (1977: 201-220). The complement-extraposition analysis is suggested by the observation that there appears to be a selectional relationship between the degree word and the degree clause:[24]

(64)a. He's so tired that he'll never get up in time.
   b. He's too tired to get up.
   c. He's tired enough to sleep 14 hours.
   d. He's as tired as he's ever been.
   e. He's (more/less) tired than you are.

However, this is not compelling evidence for an extraposition analysis over an analysis where the clause is base-generated *in situ*: there is also a close relation between determiners and relative clauses, as Abney (1987: 312-14) points out:[25]

(65)a. *the Paris
   b. the Paris that I love

Under the standard analysis of Stockwell *et al.* 1973, relative clauses are base-generated adjuncts.

In any case, it is clear that the degree clause is not head-governed at s-structure: it cannot be a specifier, as specifiers appear on the left in English and it cannot be a complement to A^0 or N^0, as there is no selectional relation between the clause and the adjective or noun head.[26] Therefore, the degree clause must be in some s-structure adjunct position, whether base-generated there or not.[27] This conclusion is not obviously reconcilable with the classical ECP account of the distribution of '*that*-deletion:' the absence of head-government should exclude null complementizers entirely.

3.4. Summary

The head-government requirement on null complementizers provides an account of the exclusion of *that*-less clauses from most non-subcategorized positions. However, it was determined that the proposed government requirement on null C^0 has the status of a stipulation. Furthermore, the account faces empirical problems: in particular, there are instances of complementizers which fulfill the structural requirements for proper government but which cannot be null (in the case of embedded sentential subjects) and there are complementizers which can be null and yet appear in positions which are not head-governed (in the case of local subject extraction, relative clauses and degree clauses). Therefore, I conclude that the loss of this analysis is not a serious objection to the IP-hypothesis.

4. EXPLAINING THE DISTRIBUTION OF IP

Under the IP-hypothesis, the problem of the distribution of *that*-less clauses is recast as the question of the distribution of IP in non-root positions. Assuming that the relevant conditions are indeed structural, the analytical task is to admit IP in complement positions on the one hand but to exclude it from subject and non-subcategorized post-verbal positions on the other:[28]

(66)a. *(That) blue jays can be annoying is obvious.
   b. It bothers me *(that) they make such a racket.

In addition, IP must be prevented from appearing in derived positions such as topicalized and extraposed positions:

(67)a. *(That) blue jays can be annoying, we all agreed.
   b. It was claimed by an independent inspection team *(that) the Sellafield nuclear plant was extremely dangerous.

Anticipating the discussion of Chapter 3 somewhat, I claim that IP can function as a relative clause in English, in the case of *that*-less relatives ('contact clauses' in terms of Jespersen 1909-49):

(68) the chest [$_{IP}$ the key opened *t*]

Therefore, an adequate account must also admit IP modifiers such as contact clauses and, if the discussion in 3.3 above is on the right track, also degree clauses.

There is one attempt (to my knowledge) at a structural account of the distribution of *that*-less clauses under the IP-hypothesis, that of Webelhuth 1992, who proposes that the categorial distinction between IP and CP is equivalent to the categorial distinction between verbs and nouns. This distinction forms the basis for an account of the distributional constraints on IP. I briefly review this proposal below, and conclude that, unfortunately, it encounters many empirical problems and incurs a certain theoretical cost.

4.1. Previous Account: Webelhuth 1992

Webelhuth assumes that verbal elements are excluded from subject position based on the observation that, in addition to CP and DP, PP is the only other category which plausibly appears in subject position:[29]

(69) Under the bed is a good place to hide.

Based on the standard assumption that DP and PP are both [-V] categories, Webelhuth proposes the following principle (Webelhuth 1992: 90):

(70) *The External Argument Universal*

External arguments are nonverbal, i.e. [-V].

Assuming that IP is verbal while CP is nominal, only the latter is predicted to appear in subject position. As further evidence for the validity of this approach, Webelhuth cites the exclusion of verb second word order (V2) from subject clauses, as illustrated in the German examples below.

(71)a. Ich glaube, [daβ Hans krank gewesen ist]
I believe that Hans sick been is

b. Ich glaube [Hans ist krank gewesen]
I believe Hans is sick been

'I believe that Hans has been sick.'

c. [*Hans ist krank gewesen] ist offensichtlich.
Hans is sick been is obvious

'That Hans has been sick is obvious.'

The standard analysis of V2 in the Government and Binding tradition is that V^0 undergoes head-movement to C^0 (see Vikner 1991, 1995 and references) with concomitant movement of an XP to the specifier position of CP. Adopting this approach, the exclusion of V2 clauses from subject position is expected. Clauses with V2 are categorially verbal, as their head position (C^0) is occupied by V^0. Therefore, they are excluded from subject position by the External Argument Universal above.

As for the apparent failure of IP to undergo syntactic movement, Webelhuth argues that this is the result of a conspiracy between the verbal nature of IP and a principle which states that moved clauses must leave nominal traces (Webelhuth 1992: 94):

(72) *The Sentence Trace Universal*

Sentences can only bind DP-traces, i.e. traces with the categorial specification [+N, -V].

A variety of evidence is provided to support this principle. For example, Webelhuth points out that verbs which reject nominal but admit clausal complements do not allow the clausal argument to become a derived subject.[30] This is illustrated for raising, unaccusative and passive verbs in the examples below.

(73)a. It seemed that John was unqualified.
b. *It seemed DP.
c. *That John was unqualified seemed [$_{DP}$ *t*].

(74)a. It turned out that John was unqualified.
b. *It turned out DP.
c. *That John was unqualified turned out [$_{DP}$ *t*].

(75)a. It was objected that John was unqualified.
  b. *It was objected DP.
  c. *That John was unqualified was objected [$_{DP}$ *t*].

If moved sentences obligatorily leave nominal (DP) traces, then raising the clausal argument to subject position necessarily leads to a violation of the selectional requirements of these verbs. Note that verbs like *expect* take both nominal and clausal complements and permit their argument clause to externalize under passive, as illustrated below.

(76)a. We expect that John will win.
  b. We expect an easy win.
  c. *That John would be unqualified* had been expected [$_{DP}$ *t*].

Assuming the Sentence Trace Universal (STU), the clause leaves a nominal trace, as illustrated above, which is consistent with the selectional requirements of the verb in this case.

Other evidence for the STU comes from the observation that the 'Internal NP over S' constraint (Ross 1967) is ameliorated when the offending embedded clause is raised to matrix subject position:

(77)a. John believes [*that Bill is sick* to be obvious].
  b. *That Bill is sick*, John believes [$_{DP}$ *t*] to be obvious.

The embedded sentential subject *in situ* is relatively ungrammatical for many speakers. However, topicalization of the embedded clause, leads to a marked improvement, as in (77)b above. This is unexpected unless the moved clause leaves a nominal trace: as discussed above, only non-verbal phrases can appear in subject position.

Furthermore, Webelhuth proposes that if movement-derived chains are uniform with respect to nominal and verbal features, as stated in (78) below, then IP-movement can be excluded in principle and the failure of extraposition and topicalization of IP receives an explanation (Webelhuth 1992: 93).

(78) *The Uniformity Requirement on Chains*

All members of a movement chain agree in verbal and nominal features, i.e. [V] and [N].

If sentences obligatorily leave nominal traces, as the STU demands, then movement of IP always violates this principle: IP is verbal but the STU requires its trace to be nominal. Therefore, movement of IP will always lead to a categorially inconsistent chain.

This approach faces several conceptual and empirical problems, however, which I outline below. First, it seems unlikely that a uniform categorial distinction between IP and CP can be maintained, under Webelhuth's criteria. In particular, Webelhuth argues that the fact that only verbs which take both nominal and clausal complements allow their complement clauses to become derived subjects is due to the fact that clauses leave nominal traces. On the other hand, verbs such as *seem, think* etc. which admit only clausal complements, do not allow their complement clauses to move to matrix subject position under passive: this is supposed to follow from the STU and the fact that these verbs reject nominal complements.

(79)a. *That the city will be destroyed seems [$_{DP}$ _].

b. *It seems [$_{DP}$ the destruction of the city].

However, this entails that CP in the complement of *think* must be categorially distinct from CP in the complement of *believe*, the former non-nominal and the latter nominal, so as to avoid a violation of the selectional requirements of the respective verbs. If this is the case, then it seems difficult to maintain that all CPs are uniformly nominal: at least some CPs must be categorially non-distinct from IP.

More seriously, however, verbal elements do in fact appear in subject position, which is not obviously reconcilable with the External Argument Universal (EAU) above: Consider that adjective phrases (which are standardly assumed to be [+V]) appear in subject position:

(80)   [Rich and famous] is what I really want to be.

The status of the adjective phrase as a true subject (as opposed to a predicate interpreted under Reconstruction) is confirmed by the possibility of Raising:[31]

(81)   [Rich and famous] seems to be what he would like to become.

Furthermore, if the bracketed constituents in (82) below are properly regarded as small clauses with verbal predicates some further doubt is cast on the validity of the EAU.[32]

(82)a.   [Cats eating sparrows] is a disturbing sight.
   b.   [People drunk at parties] drives Melvin crazy.

Assuming that small clauses are maximal projections of the predicate, as advocated by Stowell 1980, these small clause constituents are categorially [+V]. I conclude therefore that there is reason to doubt the validity of the EAU and, by extension, Webelhuth's proposal that the verbal nature of IP is sufficient to exclude it from subject position.

Finally, the account of the failure of IP-movement crucially depends on the STU, as movement of verbal elements cannot be excluded in principle given the existence of processes such as VP-preposing. However, the theoretical status of this principle is unclear, (a point made by Webelhuth himself). In particular, the informal use of the term 'sentence' in the definition covers up a stipulative disjunction. The principle states that IP and CP leave nominal traces but it remains unexplained as to why two categorially distinct phrases are permitted to both leave non-matching, DP-traces.

I conclude, therefore, that appeal to a categorial distinction between IP and CP, whether ultimately tenable or not, unfortunately provides only a partial account of the distribution of IP, and at some theoretical cost.

4.2. A Proposal

The question remains open, therefore, as to what determines the distribution of non-root IP. Below, I suggest that the beginnings of an account may lie in the principles which determine the syntactic realization of selected semantic categories.

First, consider that the distributional constraints on IP can be captured concisely in the following statement:

(83)   Selected IP must be a complement of X^0 (C^0, V^0 ...) at all levels of representation.

That is, an IP which is a selected argument (subject or complement) must appear as the complement of a syntactic head at all levels of representation: either a complementizer or a lexical head such as (V^0, A^0 ...). The ban on IP-movement (in the case of extraposition or Topicalization) is covered by this statement: Topicalized or extraposed clauses are not head-complements in their derived positions. Crucially, this requirement holds only of argument IP, as IP can be a non-selected modifier, as in the case of relative clauses and degree clauses. The task, therefore, is to uncover some basis for this restriction which draws the necessary distinction between selected and non-selected clauses.

First, however, the question arises as to how IP is licensed in complement positions at all. In many languages, IP never appears in non-root contexts: all non-matrix clauses must be realized as CP. This suggests that the default syntactic realization of the semantic category 'Proposition' is CP in these languages: i.e. in terms of Grimshaw 1981b, its 'canonical structural realization' (CSR) is CP. However, it cannot simply be the case that the CSR of 'Proposition' in English includes IP in addition to CP. Without further qualification, this would seem to predict that IP appears in all CP-positions and the distributional constraints on IP would be lost.

The requirement that argument clauses be realized as CP is equivalent to a requirement that argument IP be realized as a complement to C^0. It is possible, therefore, that the principles which determine the syntactic realization of semantic categories demand that an IP which denotes the selected semantic entity 'Proposition' be realized as a complement to a head, X^0. In other languages, X^0 is always the functional head C^0. However, in English the requirement is satisfied by the lexical heads in addition to C^0. If this is tenable, the free alternation between IP and CP complements and the exclusion of IP from subject position straightforwardly follows.

Furthermore, assuming that selected expressions must maintain their canonical structural realization at all levels of representation, the exclusion of IP from extraposed and Topicalized clauses follows: movement to a non-complement position violates the requirement that argument IP be an X^0-complement.

In addition, this approach draws the right distinction between selected and non-selected clauses: i.e. assuming non-selected expressions are not subject to canonical structural realization requirements, nothing in principle excludes their realization as IP, rather than CP. Therefore, grammatical '*that*-deletion' in degree clauses and the use of IP as a relative clause are compatible with this line of thought.

In sum, it is descriptively correct that (argument) IP must be a head-complement (at all levels of representation) and that non-selected clauses are not subject to this requirement. I have proposed that a possible basis for an explanation of this observation lies in the principles which determine the syntactic realization of semantic categories: i.e. 'Proposition' (denoted by IP) must be a complement to a head. The difference between English and other languages like Irish and Italian is simply that English admits IP as a complement to lexical heads. This approach draws the correct distinction between selected and non-selected clauses. However, the question remains as to why selected IP is subject to this constraint: I can only venture a tentative proposal.

There is nothing to suggest that matrix declarative sentences are anything other than the category IP. Therefore, it is possibly the case that IP is exclusively the category of matrix clauses: in order to be licensed as the syntactic realization of a selected 'Proposition', this inherent property must be 'turned off'. It seems clear that a defining characteristic of matrix clauses is that they are not complements to anything. Therefore, it may be that the head-complement relation is simply a syntactic device used to license the non-root appearance of IP.

5. CHAPTER SUMMARY

This chapter provides evidence from embedded adjunction facts that the IP-hypothesis of the structure of argument clauses without *that* is more appropriate than the CP-hypothesis. Therefore, in combination with the conceptual problems facing the CP-hypothesis outlined in the introduction, a strong case can be made for the IP-hypothesis.

One possible objection to the IP-hypothesis is that it is incompatible with the ECP account of the distribution of *that*-less clauses proposed in Stowell 1981. While this is indeed the case, it was demonstrated that this classical account is problematic enough from an empirical and conceptual perspective so as to warrant the reconsideration of its success. Therefore, it was concluded that the loss of this account is not a serious objection to the IP-hypothesis. The question remains then as to what principle(s) determine the distribution of *that*-less clauses, now reanalyzed as IP. Webelhuth's account based on the claim that the categorial distinction between IP and CP is equivalent to the verbal-nominal distinction was considered and rejected. However, a tentative proposal was made that the account may lie in the principles which determine the syntactic realization of selected semantic categories.[33]

As a final point, recall from section 3.2.1 above that co-ordination of clauses with and without *that* is possible. Under the IP-hypothesis, where all *that*-less clauses are IPs, it must be the case that IP and CP are permitted to co-ordinate. At first blush, this appears to be problematic, if it is assumed that only expressions which match in categorial features can co-ordinate. However, following Grimshaw (1991, 1993), IP and CP are in fact categorially non-distinct. They are both members of the (extended) verbal projection and differ only in functional features. Therefore, the fact that they can co-ordinate is unsurprising.

Furthermore, it is well-known that the co-ordination of categorially non-matching complements is occasionally permitted just in case both conjuncts are of the same semantic type:[34]

(84)a. She doesn't know the answer or how to find out anything.
  b. She walked slowly and with great care.
  c. His father ... was well-known to the police and a devout catholic.

Argument Clauses

Therefore, even if it is assumed that IP and CP do not match categorially, their co-ordination in complement positions is not unexpected, given that they both satisfy the selectional requirements of the matrix verb.

6. APPENDIX: LEXICAL RESTRICTIONS

The central proposal of this chapter is that the phenomenon of '*that*-deletion' is simply optional complementation of finite IP. This entails that V^0, A^0 and N^0 (in predicative positions at least) admit finite IP complements:[35]

(85)a. I say (that) this is true.
 b. I'm sad (that) he's not here.
 c. It's a pity (that) he left.

However, certain lexical items, including the well-known case of 'manner of speech' verbs, are incompatible with *that*-deletion in their complement clauses:

(86)a. He chuckled *(that) you were mistaken.
 b. I'm flabbergasted *(that) he said that.
 c. It's a tragedy *(that) they died like that.

An obvious approach to these facts which becomes available under the IP-hypothesis is that certain lexical items subcategorize for CP to the exclusion of IP. However, there are some reasons to reject this approach. Much recent work (e.g. Pesetsky 1991) details the benefits of reducing category selection (c-selection) to semantic selection (s-selection). If the possibility of a selectional distinction between IP and CP is admitted to the grammar, then this entails that either (i) CP and IP do not necessarily denote the same semantic entity ('Proposition') or (ii) c-selection must be assumed. Neither of these possibilities seem very desirable. Another problem for this approach is that the following generalization holds of English:

(87) Every predicate which admits an IP complement also admits a CP complement.

Therefore, if IP and CP are distinguished for selectional purposes, it is unexplained why no predicates exclusively select IP instead of CP.[36] However, in this section I will argue that the 'complement' clauses which reject *that*-deletion are not thematic complements at all, but are syntactic adjuncts and that the failure of '*that*-deletion' simply follows from the restriction of argument IP to head-complement positions. A variety of syntactic evidence, such as islandhood, supports the analysis of these clauses as adjuncts.

6.1. A Paradox: Selected Adjunct Clauses

Consider the following verbs which reject *that*-deletion in their complement clauses:

(88) a. He grieved *(that) she never returned.
   b. They reflected *(that) they were very lucky.
   c. She gloated *(that) he had been fired.
   d. Mary screamed *(that) there was a mouse on the table.
   e. John squealed *(that) his finger was caught in the door.

There is some evidence that the clausal 'complements' to these verbs are non-thematic. Note that they are optional:

(89) She grieved, gloated, reflected, squealed ...

This is never the case with the clausal complements of verbs such as *say*, *believe* etc.:

(90) *She said, believed, maintained ...

These verbs always require a clausal complement.[37]

There is also a body of evidence indicating that these clauses are in a syntactic adjunct position. First, the complements to these verbs are islands to extraction (i.e. these are 'non-bridge' verbs in the sense of Erteschik 1973):

(91) a. *What did she grieve that John told her?
   b. *What did she gloat that Mary had to endure?
   c. *What did he reflect that they were?
   d. *What did you chuckle that he said?

If these clauses are thematic subcategorized complements, then under standard conceptions, their islandhood would remain unexplained. On the other hand, if these clauses are realized in some higher adjunct position, then their islandhood is predicted: being neither θ-marked nor L-marked, they should constitute strong islands to extraction, as do other adjuncts:

(92) *Which play$_i$ did you meet John during t_i ?

Argument Clauses

There is a further argument for the adjunct status of these clausal 'complements' which applies only to the subset of these verbs which appear with an optional indirect object PP (the manner of speech verbs): Cinque (1990: 167 n. 34, citing Kayne 1981b fn. 23) claims that the clausal complements of manner of speech verbs are realized higher in the sentence than the sister of V^0 position. This is based on evidence such as the following:

(93)a. *Who$_i$ did you say t_k to t_i [that Bill was here.]$_k$

b. Who$_i$ did you yell t_k to t_i [that Bill was here.]$_k$

Cinque assumes that the clausal complement of *say* is extraposed to clause-final position, crossing the complement PP and resulting in an illegal crossing of A´-dependencies, as schematized in (94)a below. The fact that there is no similar degradation in the case of manner of speech verbs would be explained if the base-generated position of the complement clause is higher in VP than the PP complement. In that case, no ungrammaticality is expected, as the chain consisting of the questioned object of PP and its trace and the chain consisting of the moved clause and its trace do not cross, as indicated in (94)b:

(94)a. *Wh_i CP_k

(94)b.

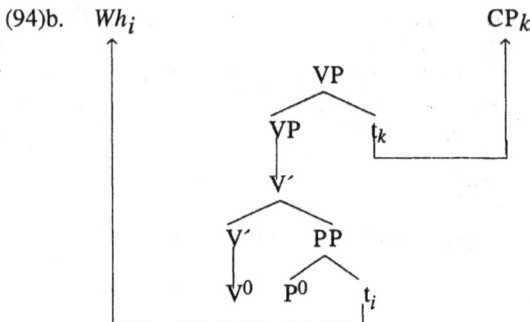

Therefore, I conclude that there is a reasonable body of evidence indicating that the complement clauses of the verbs in (88) above, and of manner of speech verbs in particular, are non-thematic syntactic adjuncts rather than thematic complements.[38]

However, this conclusion presents somewhat of a contradiction in that there is clearly a *selectional* relationship between such verbs and their clausal complement. It is not the case that finite clauses can appear with just any verb:

(95) *Mary whistled that it was time to leave.

In order to appear with a clausal complement, the verb meaning necessarily involves a speech act, as in the case of 'manner of speech' verbs or by being a verb of propositional attitude or assertion, as in the case of *believe*, *think* and *say* etc. Therefore, it is somewhat of a paradox that these clauses at once bear all the syntactic hallmarks of adjuncthood and yet are obviously semantically selected: how can a complement clause be selected and be a syntactic adjunct?

6.2. A Resolution

I propose that a resolution of this paradox is available within a more articulated theory of the relation between semantic selection and argument structure, such as that adopted in Grimshaw 1990. Grimshaw adopts the idea that verbs and nouns have associated with them a 'lexical conceptual structure' which contains, among other things, a characterization of the participants in the activities or states denoted by them. Crucially, however, the relation between semantic participants and syntactic arguments is not isomorphic: not every participant in the lexical conceptual structure is realized as a syntactic argument. Therefore, it is possible for a phrase to be at once semantically selected by an element and yet fail to be a syntactic argument: even heads completely lacking argument structure can still exert selectional requirements. Consider the examples of the nouns *book* and *gift* which lack argument structure: they are distinguished by the ability of *gift* to appear with a PP headed by *to*.

(96)a. *John's book to the hospital.
    b. John's gift to the hospital.

Grimshaw (1990: 94) proposes that it is the lexical conceptual structure of these nouns which determines the distinction: "the lexical definition of *book* ... does not include a transfer of possession, and this distinguishes *book* from *gift*." This general approach provides an explanation of the fact that derived nominals maintain the selectional requirements of their corresponding verbs. For example, the verb *attempt* is proposed to have the lexical conceptual structure in (97) below, where 'I' represents the semantic entity denoted by infinitive clauses.

(97) *attempt* (V): x attempts y (y an I)

The fact that the noun *attempt* also appears with infinitival clauses is a reflex of its lexical conceptual structure (lcs):[39]

(98) *attempt* (N): e such that x attempts y (y an I)

Grimshaw argues that in general nouns lack argument structure (see 6.3 below). Therefore, the fact that a nominal such as *attempt* can exert selectional requirements is another instance of an element without argument structure exerting selectional requirements.

This distinction between lexical conceptual and argument structure can be exploited to provide an account of the complements of manner of speech verbs such as *chuckle*. Our knowledge of what it means to chuckle tells us that it is possible to utter a sentence while in the act of chuckling. That is, these verbs are associated with an optional propositional argument in their lexical conceptual structure:

(99) *chuckle* (V): x chuckles (and utters y, y a P)

I propose that optional lcs arguments are not grammaticized as syntactic arguments. Therefore, the optional lcs argument of a non-bridge verb is present in the argument structure of the verb. I assume that only thematic arguments appear internal to VP. It follows therefore, that the non-thematic complement of a non-bridge verb is realized as a VP adjunct.

(100)
```
        VP
       /  \
      VP   CP
      |
      V'
      |
      V⁰
      |
    chuckle
```

There is some evidence that the clause is VP-adjoined. Note that the clause may not be stranded under VP-ellipsis:

(101) *Chuck groaned that he couldn't run any faster and Michael did that they had to.

This follows under the proposed analysis, if VP-ellipsis must target the largest VP, ensuring that no VP-adjuncts are stranded.[40]

The proposed analysis, in (100), resolves the paradox pointed out above: the clause is selected and yet is a syntactic adjunct. This accounts for the distinctive properties of these complement clauses. For example, the clause is optional because it is not represented in the argument structure of the verb. Furthermore, islandhood is predicted: as the clause is not a sister to V^0 it is not L-marked and as it also fails to be θ-marked it is predicted to be a barrier to both government and binding (in terms of Cinque 1990). The location of the clause higher than the normal complement position is also consistent with the crossing dependency facts outlined in (93) and (94) above. Finally, the failure of *that*-deletion is also predicted: as discussed in 4.2 above, selected IP cannot survive in non-complement positions.

The claim that optional arguments at lexical conceptual structure are not grammaticized as syntactic arguments predicts that it should be possible to predict whether a given verb takes a thematic clausal complement. If the necessary semantic 'participants' in the event or state denoted by the verb include a propositional argument, then we expect that the argument structure of the verb will represent this argument. However, if the argument is only indirectly associated or optionally present at lexical conceptual structure, then we expect the absence of a thematic argument.[41]

This approach appears to be borne out. Note that some verbs which denote a 'manner of speech' such as *shout* and *whisper* admit *that*-deletion in their complements quite readily for many speakers:

(102)a. He shouted he was about to leave.
   b. She whispered there was a snake in the house.
   c. She screamed the house was on fire.

These verbs can be interpreted as requiring a complement at lexical conceptual structure: i.e. when people shout or whisper, they mostly utter sentences or propositions. At least, the probability that these verbs are associated with a propositional complement is much higher than with verbs like *snort* or *chuckle*. In these cases, an lcs propositional argument seems entirely optional. Furthermore, the approach also seems to extend to the other non-bridge verbs: *grieve*, *gloat* etc. are only indirectly related to a propositional complement. That is, grieving and gloating have denotations independent of a propositional complement, something that is not true of verbs such as *say*, *think* etc.

This approach also extends to some other cases which Bolinger (1972: 45) terms 'verbs of physical manipulation':[42]

(103)a. He wrote *(that) it was raining in Jerusalem, but that was a scribal error.
   b. Did you record *(that) he had been rewarded?
   c. Aloud he read *(that) it was the President who had made the move.
   d. The second column repeats *(that) he is dependable.

Our knowledge of these verbs' meanings tells us that people generally read and write things: announcements, letters, sentences. However, we also know that these things are or contain (representations of) propositions. That is, the lexical conceptual structure of these verbs contains only an indirect relation to a propositional complement. Therefore, assuming that an optional lcs argument is not grammaticized, the failure of *that*-deletion in these complements is predicted.

Finally, the extension of this analysis to those adjectival and nominal predicates which reject *that*-deletion in their complements looks promising.[43] Consider the following contrasts:

(104)a. I was (overwhelmed, offended, deflated, struck, alarmed ...)*(that) he left.
   b. I was (thankful, disappointed, surprised, happy, sad ...) (that) he left.

(105)a. It was (unclear, outrageous, exhilarating, annoying...) *(that) he left.
b. It was (clear, obvious, a pity, a shame ...) (that) he left.

There is some intuitive support for this analysis and some syntactic evidence. In general, the examples in (104)a and (105)a can be used independently of a clausal complement to describe an emotional state (e.g. *I was overwhelmed*) or to describe an event (e.g. *It was outrageous*). However, this is less clear of the examples in (104-5)b which seem to primarily denote a propositional attitude. Therefore, the status of the clausal 'complements' in (104)a and (105)a as nonthematic adjuncts, analogous to manner of speech verbs, seems plausible. However, it is also true that the examples in (104-5)b can optionally denote the emotional state of the speaker (*I'm sad*, etc.).

If this analysis is on the right track, then it should be supported by extraction facts. This seems to be the case: again, as with verbal complements, there is a correlation between the ungrammaticality of *that*-deletion and syntactic islandhood:[44]

(106)a. *What were you (overwhelmed, offended ...) that he did?
b. What were you (thankful, surprised ...) that he did?

(107)a. *What was it (unclear, outrageous ...) that he did?
b. What was it (clear, a pity ...) that he did?

Therefore, I conclude that the proposed analysis of the failure of *that*-deletion in the complements of 'non-bridge' verbs may also yield an account of these cases.[45]

6.3. Noun Complement Clauses

Finally, we must consider the case of noun complement clauses. For many speakers, it seems that noun complement clauses disallow *that*-deletion:

(108)a. The hypothesis *(that) HIV was manufactured is not credible.
b. The hope *(that) he would return was unfounded.
c. The warning *(that) the bridge was unsafe went unheeded.
d. The desire *(that) no-one leave was fulfilled.
e. The plan *(that) they return home was foiled.

However, there seems to be considerable variation among speakers on this point. In particular, sentential complements to some nouns such as *fact* and *reason* seem hardly degraded at all with *that*-deletion for many speakers:

(109)a. The fact he left caused a storm.
 b. The reason he stayed wasn't apparent.

At any rate, Grimshaw 1990 provides an analysis of noun complement clauses which in combination with the general proposals of this chapter, predicts the unavailability of *that*-deletion in noun complement clauses.

Grimshaw proposes that noun complement clauses are not, in fact, θ-marked arguments of the noun.[46] One of the supporting pieces of evidence for this claim is that unlike thematic arguments, noun complement clauses appear to be optional:

(110)a. The hypothesis (that ...) is not credible.
 b. The hope (that ...) is not well-founded.
 c. The warning (that ...) was not heeded.
 d. The desire (that ...) was not fulfilled.
 e. The plan (that ...) was foiled.

There is clearly a selectional relation between the noun and the clause, however. For example, if a given verb demands a subjunctive complement, the corresponding nominal also does:

(111)a. I request that he be permitted to leave.
 b. the request that he be permitted to leave

Therefore, it is proposed that nouns take a propositional complement at the level of lexical conceptual structure but, as nouns are in general defective, this lcs argument is never grammaticized as a thematic argument. The failure of *that*-deletion in noun complement clauses then follows:

> "The fact that complementizers can never be deleted in sentential complements to nouns will follow if nouns do not theta-mark and therefore do not have the proper relationship of government to their complements." (1990: 80).

This analysis can be incorporated into a theory adopting the IP-hypothesis straightforwardly: assuming that only thematic complements appear in the sister position of a head, noun complement clauses must be realized in a higher position within the noun phrase, perhaps adjoined to NP:

(112)
```
        NP
       /  \
      NP   CP
      |
      N´
      |
      N⁰
```

Therefore, as (selected) IP must be a complement to X^0, it follows that only CPs can appear as complements to nouns. As for nouns such as *fact* and *reason* above, it could perhaps be maintained that these items actually do take thematic clausal complements. Furthermore, it might be maintained that the set of nouns which takes thematic complements is even wider in those dialects which admit *that*-deletion liberally in noun complement clauses.

However, there is perhaps some difficulty for Grimshaw's account from extraction facts. If noun complement clauses are not θ-marked, it would be expected that they function as strong islands to extraction, on a par with the complements of manner of speech verbs. However, although judgements are delicate, this is not the case. Noun complement clauses often permit extraction:

(113)a. What didn't you believe the claim that he did?
b. Who did you like the idea that they appointed?

These facts indicate that, in some cases at least, noun complement clauses may be θ-marked. However, further research is required to determine whether the possibility of extraction in these cases correlates with the possibility of *that*-deletion.

NOTES

1. Chomsky specifically proposes a phrase structure rule:

   S´´ → TOP S´

   which I have reinterpreted in more recent terms here.
2. This is an extension of the Adjunction Prohibition of Chomsky (1986a: 6) to non-movement derived adjunctions. A similar proposal is made by Rochemont (1989: 151).

3. One possibility is that the matrix present tense in (18)a and (18)b in fact is not present-time referring, but refers to near future time, in which case a matrix construal of the adverb should be possible.
4. Stowell's ECP requires government by and co-indexing with a lexical head (Stowell 1981: 381). In Stowell's system, θ-role assigners are assumed to be co-indexed with the recipient of the θ-role. As COMP is argued to be the head of S´, it bears the index of S´ which it shares with the matrix verb, because it is θ-marked by it. Therefore, null complementizers are restricted to subcategorized complement clauses, as only in this position can a complementizer be governed and co-indexed with a lexical head.
5. Pesetsky 1991 proposes that null complementizers involve syntactic movement. See 3.2.1 below.
6. This is the strict version of c-command: i.e. α c-commands β iff every branching node dominating α also dominates β.
7. The relation of m-command is the weak version of c-command i.e. a m-commands b iff. every maximal projection dominating a also dominates b.
8. Under some analyses the genitive marker *'s* is taken to be a determiner head (D^0) (see Abney 1987: 79-85 for discussion of this possibility). However, if the claim that all noun phrases (at least in argument positions) are categorially DP is adopted, then noun phrases consisting of bare plurals, bare mass nouns or proper names are necessarily analyzed as containing a phonetically null D^0 with a NP complement:

    (i)   [$_{DP}$ Ø [$_{NP}$ Geese]] are large birds.
    (ii)   [$_{DP}$ Ø [$_{NP}$ Water]] is soothing.
    (iii)   [$_{DP}$ Ø [$_{NP}$ Peter]] is here.

    These null determiners obviously cannot be subject to a proper government requirement.

    Longobardi 1991 argues for a proper government requirement on null determiners in Italian, based on the precedent of the proposed government requirement on null C^0 in English. Whatever the strength of this argument for Italian, there is no overt evidence of such a constraint in English.
9. Baker (1988: 488 n.4) also proposes a similar analysis of ECM or 'Raising to Object' verbs as an alternative to the classical S´ deletion account: following Kayne 1984, he assumes that the complement of these verbs is a CP with a null complementizer, Φ:

    I believe [$_{CP}$ Φ [$_{IP}$ him to be intelligent.]]

Incorporation of Φ into the matrix V^0 allows for the verb to govern the embedded subject by Baker's Government Transparency Corollary (the principle which permits heads which have moved from their base-generated position to govern as if they had not moved). This analysis is also adopted by Pesetsky 1991.

10. Pesetsky notes (1991: 43) that a principle such as the following may be a property of grammar:

    C^0 may not raise when phonologically overt.

    This leaves open the possibility of raising in the case of non-overt complementizers. He further suggests that at least for head-initial languages, this principle may be reflected in the existence of the 'Doubly-Filled Comp Filter' which permits either the specifier or the head of CP to be phonologically overt, but not both.

11. Thanks to Jim McCloskey and Peter Svenonius for much useful discussion about this issue.
12. However, (34) also receives an analysis as simple VP coordination.
13. These examples may not sound perfect for all speakers. Nonetheless, they are not completely ungrammatical either (*pace* Bošković 1994).
14. Thanks to Kari Swingle for useful discussion about many of the issues surrounding the RNR facts.
15. The proposal that manner of speech verbs are not proper governors also makes available an account of the failure of extraction from the complements of these verbs:

    *What did you chuckle [$_{CP}$ *t* [that he did *t*]]?

    Assuming movement proceeds through the specifier of CP, following Chomsky 1986a, the intermediate trace fails to be properly governed, as the V^0 cannot govern into the complement clause. See section 6 below for an alternative analysis of the properties of these verbs.

16. This observation is termed the 'Internal NP-over-S' Constraint in Ross 1967.
17. See Pesetsky 1991 for the alternative view that these verbs always involve CP-complementation.
18. The obvious candidate is the presence of Tense. Curiously, extraction from nonfinite sentential subjects seems more acceptable:

    Which apples would you consider [[for Mary to eat _] to be treasonous?

Thanks to Peter Svenonius for bringing this example to my attention.
19. This example is Lasnik and Saito's (96).
20. This argument depends on the analysis of prepositional elements such as *before*, *after* etc. as taking IP and not CP complements.
21. Under an *in situ* analysis of local subject extraction, as proposed by Chomsky 1986a, Grimshaw 1993 among others, this problem disappears of course. This analysis of local subject extraction is discussed extensively in Chapter 4 in relation to the head-government account of the *that*-trace effect.
22. Rizzi 1990 does not discuss the ECP analysis of the distribution of null complementizers.
23. The CP-hypothesis of the structure of *that*-less relatives would also provide an instance of an ungoverned null complementizer:

   the man [$_{CP}$ *Op* [Ø [I met t]]]

   However, as discussed extensively in Chapter 3, there is strong evidence that these clauses are simply bare IP.
24. These examples are taken from Jackendoff (1977: 201) who attributes the observation originally to Bowers 1968.
25. See also Smith 1964.
26. See Rothstein (1991: 147-154) for discussion of some of the problems for the theory of selection posed by degree clauses.
27. Abney (1987: 315) suggests that the degree clause (or 'extent clause' in his terms) is generated as sister of the degree word, in its surface position:

   [$_{DegP}$ [$_{Deg^0}$ as] [big] [as you want]]

   Although Abney does not mention the point, this proposal is consistent with the possibility of *that*-deletion in the degree clause. However, as pointed out by Abney himself, such a structure is not in keeping with current notions of phrase structure.
28. One possibility, which is not addressed here, is that the distributional constraints on *that*-less clauses may find their ultimate explanation in parsing or processing considerations. At least for sentence-initial clauses, this approach seems reasonable.
29. We will reconsider the validity of this observation presently, however.
30. This generalization is previously noted in Grimshaw 1981.
31. See Williams (1987: 444-5).
32. There is a problem for the small clause analysis of (82)a, however, in that it receives an alternative analysis as an ACC-ing construction. This analysis is supported by the fact that these constituents appear in all noun phrase positions. Therefore, it

could be argued that the constituent in (82)a is in fact categorially nominal.

However, the same analysis is clearly not available for (82)b which has an adjectival predicate. Thanks to Peter Svenonius for useful discussion about this.

33. See Svenonius 1994 (Chapter 3) for a development of the notion of dependent semantic categories.
34. See Gazdar, Klein, Pullum and Sag (1985: 174 f.) for discussion of this point. Examples (83)b and c are Gazdar *et al.*'s (10) and (11).
35. The special case of 'noun complement clauses' is discussed in 6.3 below.
36. There are a handful of expressions which seem to strongly disprefer *that*:

    (i)   Let's say (??that) we have a party.
    (ii) Suppose (??that) we have a party.

    However, it seems very unlikely that these constitute an instance of selection for a *that*-less clause. First, they are very few in number. Second, the preference for the absence of *that* is strictly limited to restricted pragmatic contexts and is not a general property of the lexical items *suppose* or *say*. Pesetsky (1991: 193-4 n. 13) makes the suggestion that these elements are simply mood markers which belong to the CP projection. This proposal seems particularly suitable to other elements which completely disallow *that* in the following clause e.g. *no wonder*:

    (iii) No wonder (*that) he's broke.
    (iv)   How come (*that) you don't know?

    I conclude that whatever their ultimate analysis, these are not instances of exclusive selection of IP by a lexical head and are not counter-examples to the generalization in (87) above. (See Bolinger (1972: 22-23) for other examples).
37. Stowell (1981: 399) argues that the failure of Topicalization or passivization also indicates that the complements of manner of speech verbs are non-thematic:

    (i)   *[That Denny was playing too much poker], which Bill muttered ...
    (ii) *[That Denny was playing too much poker] was muttered by Bill.

    However, this argument is weakened considerably by the fact that many verbs which are claimed to admit thematic clausal complements (e.g. *think*, *hope*) also fail to be comfortable to varying degrees with Topicalization or Passivization:

(i) ??That she was lying, they all thought.
(ii) ??That she was lying was thought by them all.

38. Stowell 1981 also reaches this conclusion specifically for the complements to manner of speech verbs.
39. *e* stands for event here.
40. This is suggested by the fact that adverbs which obligatorily appear left-adjoined to VP (*merely, simply*) (see Jackendoff 1977: 51) cannot be stranded under VP-ellipsis:

(i) *Mary refused to be quiet but John did simply.

On the other hand, the following cases of grammatical stranding under VP-ellipsis are plausible instances of IP-adjunction:

(ii) John got married when he was 24 and Mark did
when he was 25.

This is indicated by the independent appearance of such adverbs as IP-adjuncts:

(iii)   When he was 25, John got married.

Therefore, these adverb-stranding facts provide some positive indication that VP-ellipsis targets the largest possible constituent. Thanks to Jim McCloskey for pointing this out to me.

41. Note that proposal is a distinct one from that of Erteschik 1973. Erteschik proposes that it is the semantic complexity of verbs which determines whether their complements are syntactic islands or not. Manner of speech verbs are semantically complex because they involve a description of the speech act itself. However, under the proposed approach, 'manner of speech' verbs generally fail to take thematic complements not because they involve a manner description but because they are only optionally associated with a propositional complement.
42. These are taken from Bolinger's (unnumbered) list of examples, Bolinger (1972: 45).
43. I should point out, however, that speakers' judgements on these sentences (including my own) seem variable.
44. As with the sentences in (104) and (105), however, there is considerable variation with these judgments.
45. It is often reported that factive verbs (e.g. *regret, reveal, disclose* ...) reject *that*-deletion in their complements (McDavid 1963, Erteschik 1973, Hegarty 1991, Melvold 1991). However, the claim that factivity and *that*-deletion are directly related seems

tenuous given that many of these adjectival and nominal predicates are factive and are fully grammatical with *that*-less complements:

(i) I'm sad (that) this quarter is over.
(ii) I'm happy (that) this quarter is over.
(iii) It's a good thing (that) this quarter is over.

That these predicates are truly factive is shown by their retention of the presupposition under negation:

(iv) I'm not sad (that) this quarter is over.
(v) I'm not happy (that) this quarter is over.
(vi) It's not a good thing (that) this quarter is over.

46. She argues that nouns in general lack argument structure. The exceptions are 'complex event nominals' such as *felling* which take obligatory argument complements. However, these are never sentential complements.

CHAPTER 3

Relative Clauses

1. INTRODUCTION

This chapter argues for the IP-hypothesis of the structure of *that*-less relatives (*contact clauses* in the terms of Jespersen 1909-49):[1]

(1) He has found the key [you lost *e* yesterday.]

Previous analyses in the tradition of the Extended Standard Theory (EST) assume that this construction has exactly the structure of other restrictive relatives, differing only in that it involves a phonologically null relative operator and a null complementizer (e.g. Chomsky and Lasnik 1977):[2]

(2) the key [$_{CP}$ *which$_i$* [$_{C'}$ ø [$_{IP}$ you lost t_i]]]

(3) the key [$_{CP}$ *Op$_i$* [$_{C'}$ that [$_{IP}$ you lost t_i]]]

(4) the key [$_{CP}$ *Op$_i$* [$_{C'}$ ø [$_{IP}$ you lost t_i]]]

The absence of a complementizer or relative pronoun makes no discernible semantic difference. Therefore, this analysis is compatible with the complete synonymy of contact clauses and other restrictive relative clauses.

However, contact clauses are distinguished from (other) relative clauses by a number of syntactic properties. In particular, they are subject to a strong adjacency requirement: they fail to 'stack' or to undergo 'extraposition from NP'. The earliest generative analyses of contact clauses classified them among the set of postnominal modifiers, along with expressions such as *willing to learn*, *able to help*: i.e. the output of the classical 'relative clause reduction' transformation (Smith

1964). This approach is insightful in that many postnominal modifiers are also subject to similar adjacency requirements. However, under the EST assumption that contact clauses are structurally identical to other relative clauses, this restriction is not obviously captured.

In this chapter, I provide novel empirical evidence that contact clauses are structurally distinct from other relative clauses. I argue from adjunction facts that they do not contain a CP projection. On that basis, I propose that they are simply IP postnominal modifiers which directly modify a noun phrase without the apparatus of syntactic operator movement.[3] Specifically, I propose that the contact clause is an adjunct to NP and that it involves an A´-chain which directly links the relative head (the NP to which relative modifiers are attached) with a (base-generated) empty category in the gap position:

(5) the [$_{NP}$ [$_{NP}$ key$_i$] [$_{IP}$ you lost e_i]]

This analysis at once accounts for the similarities between contact clauses and full relative clauses and forms the basis for an account of the syntactic peculiarities of the former, such as the adjacency restriction.

A further difference between contact clauses and other (full) relative clauses is that contact clauses with subject gaps are generally ungrammatical:

(6) *The key opens the chest is missing.

However, it is well-known that under poorly-understood conditions, a construction which is at least string-identical with subject contact clauses does appear:

(7) There's a girl (who) wants to see you.
(8) I knew a smart Greek fella (who) owns maybe twenty restaurants.
(9) It was Bill (who) did it.

The restricted distribution of examples such as this is often claimed to indicate that, despite appearances, these are not subject-gap contact clauses but are some other construction (e.g. Erdmann 1980). In this chapter, I provide novel evidence to the contrary and claim that examples such as (7)-(9) do in fact instantiate contact clauses with subject gaps (subject contact clauses). Furthermore, I claim that their distributional characteristics follow directly from the proposed classification of contact clauses as postnominal modifiers lacking the apparatus of syntactic operator-movement.

The structure of the chapter is as follows. In the following section, the syntactic properties of contact clauses are outlined in more detail. In section 2, evidence is provided for the IP-hypothesis of the structure of contact clauses and the proposal that they lack operator-movement is outlined. Section 3 argues for the existence of subject-gap contact clauses and section 4 addresses the question of their distribution.

1.1. Syntactic Properties of Contact Clauses

It is characteristic of restrictive relatives that they 'stack': i.e. appear recursively after the modified noun:[4]

(10)a. the man who Mary met who John likes
   b. the book that Bill bought that Max wrote
   c. the book which Bill bought that Mary disliked

Notably, however, contact clauses must appear immediately adjacent to the modified noun phrase. Only the first clause of a stacked structure can be a contact clause. They cannot be separated from the relative head by another clause:

(11)a. the man Mary met who John likes
   b. *the man Mary met John likes
   c. the book Bill bought that Max wrote
   d. *the book Bill bought Max wrote

Secondly, this adjacency constraint is also apparent in that contact clauses cannot undergo 'extraposition from NP' unlike restrictive relatives with overt complementizers or relative pronouns:[5]

(12)a. John gave a book (that) he wrote to Mary.
   b. John gave a book to Mary that he wrote
   c. *John gave a book to Mary he wrote.

(13)a. A moose (that) Bill shot at appeared.
   b. A moose appeared that Bill shot at.
   c. *A moose appeared Bill shot at.

(14)a. The man *(who) Bill knew* arrived yesterday.
   b. The man arrived yesterday *who Bill knew*.
   c. *The man arrived yesterday *Bill knew*.

Given these facts, the following generalization can be stated of contact clauses (revealing the aptness of Jespersen's term):

(15) Contact clauses must be adjacent to the noun phrase they modify.

Another obvious difference between contact clauses and other relative clauses is that pied-piping is available only in the latter:

(16)a. the man I gave a book to [$_{DP}$ *e*]

b. the man [$_{CP}$ to whom [$_{IP}$ I gave a book [$_{DP}$ *e*]]]

c. *the man to I gave a book [$_{PP}$ *e*]

If contact clauses involve movement of an operator to specifier of CP then it might be expected that they too should admit pied-piped structures.[6]

Finally, subject-gap contact clauses are licensed only in very restricted circumstances, as noted above. This is obviously not the case for relative clauses with overt complementizers or relative pronouns. This too suggests that there may be a significant structural difference between contact clauses and (full) restrictive relatives.

On the other hand, there are also strong similarities between contact relatives and other restrictive relative clauses. As noted in the introduction, there is no discernible interpretive difference between contact clauses and the corresponding full relative clauses. More significantly, contact clauses freely conjoin with other relative clauses, as illustrated below:

(17)a. The man John likes and who Mary can't stand walked in.
b. The man John likes and that can't stand Mary walked in.
c. The man who John likes and Mary can't stand walked in.
d. The man that John likes and Mary dislikes intensely walked in.

In conclusion, it seems that contact clauses have all the semantic properties of restrictive relative clauses and also some of their syntactic properties.[7] A successful analysis of this construction must at once account for these significant differences and similarities.

Before addressing the question of the structure of contact clauses, however, it seems necessary to fix some assumptions as to the structure and interpretation of relative clauses.

1.2. Restrictive Relative Clauses: Assumptions

I assume that relative clause modifiers are property-denoting expressions, predicates derived from sentences.[8] Their interpretation is such that the gap corresponds to a variable bound by a λ-operator:

(18)a. the man *that Mary likes e*

b. λx[like´(Mary, x)]

In the tradition of the Extended Standard Theory it is assumed that the syntactic correlate of the λ-abstraction is a syntactic A´-chain, i.e. a syntactic operator in the leftmost position of the clause (corresponding to the λ-operator) binds an empty category (corresponding to a variable). In *wh*-relatives this operator is overt: it is the relative pronoun. In other relatives it is assumed to be phonologically null, as in (2)-(4) above. Under the standard assumption that restrictive clause modifiers adjoin to the modified noun phrase, the structure of a relative clause is as follows:[9]

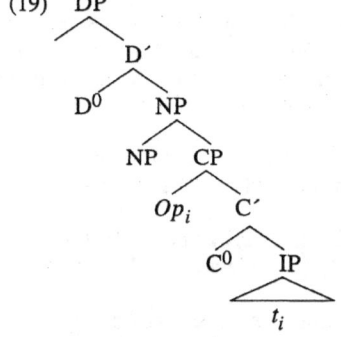

Some mechanism is required to connect the relative clause modifier to the relative head under this approach. This mechanism is typically assumed to be a binding relation, as in Safir 1986, who claims that the binding relation between the relative head and the operator in the relative modifier (which he terms 'R-Binding') is A-binding, distinct from the A´-binding relation between the relative operator and the variable ('X-Binding'). In the general case, the variable in the clause is both R-bound and X-bound. However, in pied-piped constructions, the two binding relations necessarily diverge:

(20) the key$_j$ [[with which$_j$]$_i$ [you opened the chest t_i]]

In these cases, the syntactically bound variable (t_i) is not directly bound by the relative head.

2. THE STRUCTURE OF CONTACT CLAUSES

I present evidence below which indicates that contact clauses should be properly regarded as bare IP, rather than CP with a null head. However, as clauses normally require some kind of syntactic operator-variable chain in order to receive an interpretation as a property-denoting expression, it is initially paradoxical that contact clauses lack a CP-level. This is especially true given the strong syntactic evidence for the presence of an A´-chain in contact clauses, discussed in 2.2 below. I propose, however, that this paradox is resolved if the relative head (the NP to which relative clauses attach) is permitted to directly A´-bind a variable in the gap-position. This analysis is then shown to provide an account of many of the syntactic properties of contact relatives.

2.1. Contact Clauses are IP

Note that relative clauses reject adverbial adjunction on a reading where the adverb is construed within the relative clause. For this construal to be possible, the adverb must appear to the right of the complementizer or relative pronoun, presumably adjoined to the IP level:

(21)a. *the officers evidently who the rioters assaulted
    b. the officers who evidently the rioters assaulted

    c. *the man clearly who the highway patrol assaulted
    d. the man who clearly the highway patrol assaulted

The explanation for this effect is not immediately obvious. However, it may reduce to a general prohibition against adjunction to adjunct clauses. As illustrated in the following example, adjunct clauses seem to reject adjunction (McCloskey (1992: 12)):

(22) *I graduated [while at college [without having really learned anything]].

Whatever the ultimate explanation, this fact provides a useful probe into the syntax of the left-edge of relative clause modifiers. Under the assumption that contact clauses are structurally identical to relative clauses, as in (4) above, it would be expected that they allow adverbial

Relative Clauses

adjunction to the right of the null complementizer, as illustrated schematically below.

(23) NP [$_{CP}$ *Op* [$_{C'}$ ø [$_{IP}$ *Adverb* [$_{IP}$ ...]]]]

However, this prediction is not borne out: the intervention of any material at all between the relative head and the contact clause results in severe ungrammaticality:

(24) a. That's the man *(who) years ago Mary used to know well.
  b. That's the woman *(who) tomorrow we'll meet after lunch.
  c. This is the woman *(who) most of the time John likes.
  d. There's the man *(who) just this morning I met in the shop.

Under the classical EST approach, there is no obvious account for this restriction. Adverbial adjunction to the IP-level can have no bearing on whether the complementizer is realized as *that* or ø. However, if the facts in (21) above show that adverbial adjunction to relative clause modifiers is excluded in principle, then the exclusion of adjunction to contact clauses is explained if the maximal projection of the contact clause modifier is IP, rather than CP. Assuming that contact clause modifiers appear in the same syntactic position as other relative clauses, the structure of contact clauses is as follows:

(25)
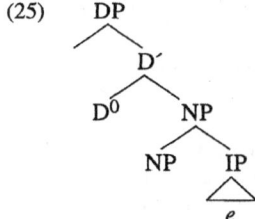

This structure gives rise to an immediate concern, however: under the assumption that syntactic operator-variable chains are necessary for clauses to be interpreted as property-denoting expressions, it is not obvious how this structure can be interpreted as a relative clause, given the absence of a standard A'-chain linking a relative operator and a variable in the relativized position.

2.2. The A´-Chain in Contact Clauses

There is strong evidence that contact clauses contain a syntactic A´-chain. A´-chains are classically defined by the following diagnostics of Chomsky 1977 and other work:

(26) A´-Chains:

    (i)   terminate in an obligatory gap
    (ii) are apparently unbounded
    (iii) obey Subjacency

The gap in an A´-chain:

    (iv) licenses parasitic gaps (Engdahl 1981)
    (v) is subject to Strong Crossover
    (vi) is subject to Weak Crossover (Safir 1986)

These characteristics hold of the operator-gap chain in relative clauses and are respectively illustrated in the following examples.[10]

(27)a. *the man who that you saw him/John
    b. the man that you said that you thought that you knew t
    c. *the guy that you believed the rumor that John hated t
    d. the guy that you judged t without really knowing pg
    e. *the man$_i$ who$_i$ he$_i$ thinks t_i is intelligent
    f. *the man$_i$ who$_i$ his$_i$ mother thinks t_i is intelligent

The same characteristics are typical of contact clauses:

(28)a. *the man you saw him/John
    b. the man you said you thought you knew t
    c. *the guy you believed the rumor that John hated t
    d. the guy you judged without really knowing t
    e. *the man$_i$ he$_i$ thinks t_i is intelligent
    f. *the man$_i$ his$_i$ mother thinks t_i is intelligent

Therefore, these properties strongly suggest that contact clauses contain a syntactic A´-chain. However, it is not immediately clear how these observations can be accommodated into an analysis of contact clauses as bare-IPs.

There seem to be two possibilities: (i) contact clauses contain a standard A´-chain derived through syntactic movement of a null operator to some (IP-internal) operator position; (ii) the A´-chain is derived without syntactic movement. These possibilities are explored in turn below and the latter is proposed to be superior.

2.2.1. *The Null Operator Approach*

There seem to be two potential locations for a null operator in IP-relatives: IP-adjunct position, as in (29)a below, or specifier of some Operator Phrase, intermediate between IP and CP, as in (29)b below.[11]

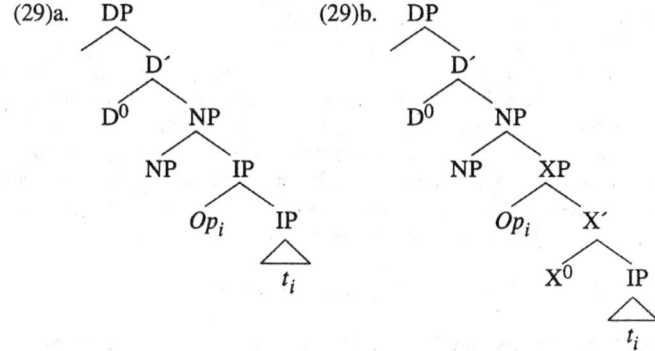

Any analysis along these lines straightforwardly accounts for the fact that contact clauses display all the diagnostics for A´-chains as do (full) relatives: both constructions are derived through syntactic movement of an operator to clause-initial position.

In addition, this approach is consistent with the observation that contact clauses co-ordinate freely with (full) relative clauses. If the possibility of co-ordination of semantically identical phrases is permitted, despite a categorial difference, then it would be expected that contact clauses and relative clauses co-ordinate, as all the indications are that there is no semantic difference between the two constructions. Alternatively, if IP and CP are categorially non-distinct, following Grimshaw (1991, 1993) the possibility of co-ordination is also predicted, assuming that co-ordination possibilities are determined by strict categorial matching.[12]

Furthermore, the failure of pied-piping follows, adopting the standard assumption that null operators are morphologically [-*wh*], i.e. they do not license an expression in which they are embedded to function as an operator:

(30) *a man [$_{CP}$ to Op_i [$_{C'}$ ∅ [$_{IP}$ I gave a book [$_{PP}$ t_i]]]]

This morphological property of null operators ensures that the gap is necessarily nominal.

However, there is a major problem for this approach in that it is not clear how the failure of adverbial adjunction can be predicted. If operator-adjunction to the IP is permitted, as in (29)a, it is unclear why adverbial adjunction is also not permitted. If a CP projection prevents IP from being the maximal projection of the relative clause modifier, as in (29)b, then it is not obvious how the failure of adverbial adjunction to contact relatives can be accounted for.[13]

Given these problems, it seems unlikely that any analysis in terms of null operator movement could be sufficiently distinct from the classical EST analysis to provide an explanation of the adjunction facts discussed in 2.1 above. Finally, this approach does not offer much hope of an account of the adjacency restriction on contact clauses: as *that*-relatives are also assumed to involve null operator movement, yet are not subject to any adjacency restrictions, it is unlikely that the restriction follows from some property of null operators.

2.2.2. Proposal: A´-Chains without Movement

The alternative is that contact clauses lack syntactic operator movement entirely and that the relative head itself (the NP to which restrictive modifiers are adjoined) directly binds an empty category in the relativized position:

(31)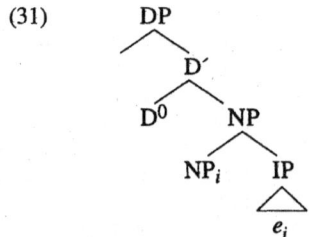

Under this approach, the evidence that contact clauses contain a syntactic A´-chain is accounted for, assuming that the relative head is classified among the set of A´-positions. This proposal does not seem problematic: under standard conceptions, an A´-position is one which can never bear a θ-role, the canonical example being specifier of CP. On the other hand, A-positions are those which possibly do bear a θ-role (even if they actually do not, e.g. the subject of a passive or unaccusative verb). Clearly, the relative head is plausibly classified as an A´-position by this definition. It is the entire noun phrase, the DP node which enters into thematic relations with external elements, not the relative head itself.[14]

In the minimalist framework of Chomsky (1992: 40f.), the distinction between A and A´ positions is recast in terms of the notion of 'lexical relatedness' (L-relatedness). A position is L-related if it is in a local structural relation with a head bearing an 'L-feature': i.e. features which must be realized on lexical heads (e.g. Tense, Agreement). A position is narrowly L-related if it is the specifier or complement (in the checking or internal domain) of such a head. Positions which are not at all L-related are equated with A´-positions. By this definition, the relative head in (31) above cannot be classified as an A-position, as it is not narrowly L-related to any element.

Therefore, in both the classical theory and in the minimalist framework, the relative head is plausibly classified among the set of A´-positions. Therefore, the proposal that the relative head directly A´-binds the gap in the contact clause does not seem problematic. As for the nature of the empty category in the gap position, I assume that it is simply a base-generated phonologically null variable.[15] Therefore, I conclude that the proposed analysis is consistent with current assumptions as to the syntax and interpretation of relative clauses.

2.3. The Adjacency Restriction

This analysis also provides the basis for a plausible syntactic account of the adjacency restriction noted in (15) above. I assume that an A´-chain consists of an operator which c-commands a co-indexed variable in an A-position. Under this assumption, it is clear that if the contact clause is extraposed, the A´-binding relation between the relative head and the gap in the relativized position cannot be maintained. Under the assumption that the integrity of this binding relation is required, the failure of extraposition with contact clauses is expected. This result obtains whether extraposed contact clauses are adjoined to VP or to the matrix level, as illustrated below.[16]

(32)a. *IP   (32)b. *IP

[tree diagrams]

In either case, the c-command relation between the relative head and the relative clause fails.[17] Full relatives (CP-relatives), on the other hand, are not subject to any such restriction because the variable in the relativized position is A´-bound within the clause itself and is not dependent on direct binding from the relative head.

As for stacked relatives, these are plausibly excluded by a couple of considerations. Assuming (following Stockwell *et al.* 1973: 442) that stacked relatives are attached recursively to the modified noun phrase, stacked contact relatives should have the following structure:

(33)
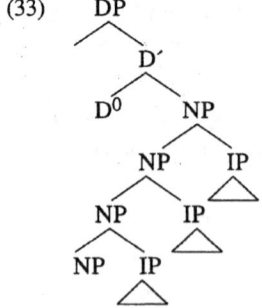

In this structure, the relative head would necessarily directly bind the gap in each stacked relative. However, it is not clear that the above structure could admit this binding relation in any but the adjacent relative clause, as under the strictest version of c-command the relative head could only bind into this clause and none of the others.[18]

Secondly, however, another factor straightforwardly excludes this structure: i.e. the Bijection Principle of Koopman and Sportiche (1982: 146):

(34)   *The Bijection Principle*

There is a bijective correspondence between variables and A´-positions.

That is, every variable is locally bound by one and only one A´-operator and every A´-operator binds one and only one A-position. Clearly, if something like the Bijection Principle constrains A´-binding, stacked IP-relatives should be excluded under the proposed analysis.[19] On the other hand, the empty category in other relatives is bound within the relative clause modifier itself by a A´-operator in specifier of CP. Therefore, no restriction on the stacking of CP-relatives is expected.

Another explanation for the adjacency constraint under the classical EST analysis of contact clauses is suggested in Aoun *et al.* (1987: 575) who argue that it is a reflex of the same constraint which is alleged to account for the distribution of null complementizers in complement clauses: i.e. null elements are proposed to be subject to a requirement of lexical government at Phonological Form (PF). Therefore, the failure of stacked structures such as the following is due to the non-adjacency of the contact clause to a lexical governor:

(35)   The story (that) Fay wrote *(that) *The Nation* published was about the FBI.

Under their assumptions, deleted complementizers leave a residue which is visible at PF and requires lexical government (i.e. string adjacency to a lexical head). However, null complementizers are also present in *wh*-relatives.

(36)   the housemate [$_{CP}$ who$_i$ [$_{C'}$ ø [$_{IP}$ I dislike t_i intensely]]]

It is not clear, under their proposal, why the null complementizer which appears in this construction is not subject to the same requirements as that assumed to be present in contact clauses.

2.4. Summary

In conclusion, it has been proposed that contact clauses are bare IP relative clauses which lack syntactic operator movement and that the relative head directly A´-binds the gap. This analysis straightforwardly explains the syntactic and semantic similarities between contact and other restrictive relatives. Note that the analysis is also compatible with the fact that contact clauses and full CP-relatives can freely co-ordinate, as illustrated in (17) above. I assume that co-ordination possibilities are determined by semantic in addition to syntactic factors i.e. phrases which denote semantically similar entities can co-ordinate.[20]

Under this assumption, the co-ordination of contact clauses and CP-relatives is not unexpected: all the indications are that contact clauses and CP-relatives denote the same semantic entity.

Furthermore, the analysis provides the basis for a plausible structural analysis of the adjacency restriction. I argue that this is a distinct advantage of the present analysis over previous accounts. Under the classical EST assumption that contact clauses have the same syntactic structure as other restrictive relatives, it is not clear how this restriction could be accounted for. Under the standard assumption that null operators are present in *that*-relatives, it is unlikely that the adjacency requirement on contact clauses is a property of null operators, as *that*-relatives are not subject to any distributional restrictions. Therefore, the proposed analysis meets the criteria outlined in 1.1 above: it accounts for the differences between contact clauses and full relative clauses and yet predicts their strong similarities.

The crucial distinction between contact and full CP-relatives is the absence of syntactic operator-movement in contact clauses and the presence of direct binding from the relative head into the relativized position. In this sense, contact clauses are classified among the set of postnominal modifiers (expressions such as *aware of our difficulties*, *able to help* etc.) i.e. so-called 'reduced relatives', the output of the classical 'relative clause reduction' transformation (Smith 1964). These expressions are also restrictive modifiers, an argument of which is identified with the denotation of the modified noun phrase, presumably through a binding or Control relation. It is therefore unsurprising that such expressions are subject to the same adjacency restrictions as contact clauses. Note that in general, they cannot extrapose or stack:

(37) a. Anybody [able to help] is welcome.
　　 b. *Anybody is welcome [able to help.]

(38) a. John is a man [able to help.]
　　 b. *John is a man [able to help] [aware of our difficulties.]

An obligatory binding relation between the modified noun phrase and an argument within the modifier would ensure that stacking and extraposition are excluded along the lines outlined for contact clauses above. This classification also forms the basis for an understanding of the distributional constraints on subject contact clauses, as argued in following sections.

3. SUBJECT CONTACT CLAUSES

It is well-known that in informal or colloquial speech, subject contact clauses are licensed in certain syntactic environments, as in the following examples:[21]

(39)a. There's a girl wants to see you.
   b. Was it him did it?
   c. That's the girl wanted to see you yesterday.
   d. I knew someone years ago used to do that.

This construction is not restricted to any geographical dialect: the data in this chapter comes variously from North American, British and Hiberno-English.[22] Despite the considerable traditional and descriptive literature on this topic (e.g. Auwera 1984, Erdmann 1980, Nagucka 1980 and references therein) this construction has received little attention in the generative tradition.

The common observation is that the syntactic distribution of the construction is very limited. In the majority dialect it seems to appear only in existential and copular sentences, as reported in Erdmann 1980, Jespersen 1909-49 and others. This restricted distribution has prompted claims that contact clauses with subject gaps do not exist, and that the apparent instances of the construction in (39) above represent some 'looser' form of predication. This claim has been advanced by Erdmann 1980, and most recently by McCawley (1981, 1988). However, in the following sections it is argued that the constructions in (39) above do in fact instantiate subject-gap contact relatives.

I furthermore argue that the proposed analysis of contact clauses is consistent with the restricted distribution of subject contact clauses. Novel evidence is provided that the distribution of the construction is wider than has been traditionally observed. Supported by these observations, I argue that the distributional properties of subject contact clauses are not unique to the construction at all but are typical of many other postnominal modifiers with missing subjects.

3.1. Distribution: The Majority Dialect

The general consensus in the traditional literature is that subject contact clauses are most frequently encountered in existential and copular sentences. For example, Jespersen (1909-49: 148) remarks that all the sentence-types in which subject contact clauses are licensed contain some 'meaningless existential element.' More precisely, subject contact clauses most commonly appear in copular and *have*-existentials, *it*-clefts and other copular sentences with deictic subjects:

Copular Existentials
- (40)a. There's something keeps upsetting him. (Q959)
  - b. There's nobody living now has this song but myself. (LN71)
  - c. There isn't one of us really knows what she's doing it for. (C235).

Have Existentials
- (41)a. I have this friend lives in Dublin.
  - b. I have an idea might work.
  - c. You get people in Green Park have never set foot in Battersea Park and *vice versa*. (E142)

It-Clefts
- (42)a. It was our laughter stung him worst. (GF43)
  - b. It was Bill did it.
  - c. It's money makes the world go round.

Other Copular Sentences
- (43)a. Is that the boy was causing all the bother?
  - b. Here's the one'll get it for you.
  - c. That's the fella was breaking stones on the altar. (GF49)

In addition, the construction often appears in the complement of *know*, when introducing an individual into a discourse.

- (44)a. I know a smart Greek fella owns maybe twenty restaurants. (W19)
  - b. I know a fella can get all the tobacco he wants: Frank Dooley ... (GF102)

However, as is frequently noted in the literature, the distribution of the construction is extremely limited: it seems to be generally excluded from subject position and from the complement positions of predicates other than the above (see Bolinger 1972: 11; Lodge 1979: 183, respectively):

(45)a. *The man worked there was a friend of mine.
 b. *I gave a ticket to a man comes every day.

It is unlikely that the unacceptability of examples such as (43) is due to parsing difficulties, often claimed to exclude examples such as (46):

(46) the horse raced past the barn fell

This is because there are occasional examples of sentence-initial subject contact clauses. For example, Chomsky and Lasnik (1977: 428) point out the following example from African American Vernacular English:[23]

(47) the man own the land come over.

To this we can add the following example of a fronted predicate nominal, which seems less dialectal:

(48)a. John is the only one can do it.
 b. The only one can do it is John.

Therefore, the ungrammaticality of examples such as (45) cannot reflect the operation of some universal ban on sentence-initial subject contact clauses.[24] These facts are discussed further in section 3.4 below.

3.2. Subject Contact Clauses as non-Relative Clauses

This restricted distribution has led to claims that these apparent instances of subject contact clauses are in reality a distinct construction. This position is taken by many in the traditional literature, as reported by Erdmann (1980: 161), who himself proposes that subject contact clauses are not subordinate clauses but are an instance of 'main clause juxtaposition without a connective.'[25] A variant of this claim has been most recently proposed by McCawley (1981, 1988) and is examined in detail below.

McCawley argues for the existence of a class of *pseudo-relatives* which, though string-identical to restrictive relative clauses, are structurally distinct from them in that the relative clause modifier is external to the modified noun phrase.[26] As the environments in which pseudo-relatives appear seem identical to the licensing environments for subject contact clauses, McCawley suggests that the omission of a subject relative marker unambiguously encodes the pseudo-relative structure.

Two main pieces of syntactic evidence for the existence of pseudo-relatives are provided. First, noting that parenthetical insertion between a noun phrase and a restrictive relative clause modifier is generally ungrammatical (as illustrated in (49) below), McCawley points out that this is not the case in the specific contexts given in (50):

(49)a. *Fred was just talking to the person incidentally who asked John for help.
  b. *Dorothy arrived in the day of course when I was in Toledo.

(50)a. There are many Americans, of course, who distrust politicians.
  b. Paul has a brother, incidentally, who lives in Toledo.
  c. Nixon is the only president, as you know, who ever resigned.
  d. I've never met an American, by the way, who didn't like pizza.

On this basis, it is argued that the relative clause modifier is external to the modified noun phrase in these constructions: i.e. they do not form a complex noun phrase with the nominal they modify.

The second piece of evidence supporting this proposal comes from extraction facts: extraction from pseudo-relatives in many cases leads only to a mild degree of ill-formedness, which would be unexpected if the clause was internal to the modified noun phrase. In that case, a Complex Noun Phrase Constraint (CNPC) violation should ensue, which is characteristically severely ungrammatical (McCawley 1988: 428):[27]

(51)a. ?Which persons do you think there are many Americans who distrust?
  b. ??What company does John have a brother who works for?
  c. ?How many exam papers is Smith the only instructor who hasn't read yet?
  d. Which foods have you never met an American who doesn't like?

The following are attested spontaneous examples.

Relative Clauses

(52) a. This is the one that Bob Wall was the only person who hadn't read.
b. Then you look at what happens in languages that you know and languages that you have a friend who knows.
c. It's a distinction which I'm sure I'm the only person in the world who has.

Therefore, as the licensing domain for pseudo-relatives seems identical to that of subject contact clauses, McCawley suggests that the absence of a relative marker in subject-gap relatives may simply encode the pseudo-relative structure. However, before considering this proposal in more detail, some independent evidence for the existence of the pseudo-relative structure is presented below.

3.2.1. Independent Evidence for the Pseudo-relative Construction

There is considerable independent evidence for the existence of pseudo-relative structures. Restricting our attention initially to the copular existential construction, there is strong evidence that the postcopular DP and the predicate phrase in the coda position (henceforth, the XP) do not form a complex noun phrase i.e. the XP is necessarily outside the DP, as indicated below.

(53) There is [$_{DP}$ a unicorn] [$_{XP}$ in the garden].

The evidence for this claim is to be found in Barwise and Cooper 1981 and Keenan 1987 and is summarized in McNally 1992 along with additional arguments. I present only the main points here. First, the postcopular material in existential sentences often cannot appear in canonical noun phrase positions, such as subject position. This is illustrated in the following examples.[28]

(54) a. There are two students who object to that enrolled in the course.
b. There is a woman who knows you working at the Pub these days.
c. There was nobody but Mitzi interested in that movie.

(55) a. *Two students who object to that enrolled in the course just came in.
b. *A woman who knows you working at the Pub these days just won the lottery.
c. *Nobody but Mitzi interested in that movie will be at the theater.

A second argument for the DP-external location of the XP predicate is that question formation and comparative deletion can target the postcopular DP, stranding the predicate phrase:[29]

(56) a. Who is there performing at the Academy this week?
b. The new mall ruined the few businesses there were still functioning downtown.
c. There are more students voting for the environmental initiative than there are voting against it.

This is not the case if extraction or comparative deletion targets the same phrases when in a post-nominal modifier position. In this case, severe ungrammaticality results:

(57) a. *Who do the musicians admire performing at the Academy this week?
b. *The businesses to which the city has given a tax break still functioning downtown are in greater danger than ever.
c. ??The lobby endorsed more candidates supporting gun control than they did opposing it.

This indicates that the XP is external to the postcopular DP in the existential.

McNally provides another argument based on the licensing of Negative Polarity Items (NPI). She notes that NPIs are licensed by *every* only within the DP headed by it, as illustrated below.[30]

(58) a. Everyone with any money has bought a VCR; why haven't you?
b. *Everyone has any money.

However, the postcopular material in existential sentences does not behave like a complex DP in this respect: *every* in the postcopular DP *cannot* license an NPI in the XP, as illustrated below. The first example is ungrammatical and the second allows only 'free-choice' *any* in the coda, not the NPI reading:

(59) a. *There is every breed of dog with any chance of winning competing in any competition.
b. There is every kind of music that anyone can imagine available on any jukebox.

Again, this serves to indicate that the post-copular material in the existential is not a complex DP. Therefore, it seems clear that whatever the correct syntactic structure of existential sentences, the XP predicate is outside the projection of the postcopular DP.[31]

Given the grammaticality of sentences such as the following, it must be the case that relative clauses can fill the XP slot:

(60) There was [$_{DP}$ only John] [$_{XP}$ that Mary got along with.]

The relative clause cannot be parsed as part of the post-copular DP in this example: *only John that Mary got along with* is not a well-formed noun phrase. Therefore, McCawley's class of pseudo-relatives seems well-motivated, at least for existential sentences: relative clauses can appear external to the modified noun phrase in this construction.

The question arises then, if there is independent evidence for pseudo-relatives in the other positions in which subject contact clauses appear. The answer is clearly affirmative in the case of *it*-clefts and *have*-existentials. The post-copular material in the cleft and post-verbal material in the *have*-existential do not necessarily form a constituent which can appear in canonical noun phrase positions. This is illustrated below:

(61)a. It was Bill who did it.
   b. You get plenty of that type who live around here.

(62)a. *Bill who did it was chastised thoroughly.
   b. *Plenty of that type who live around here cause many problems for the residents.

Therefore, McCawley's claim that the relative clauses which appear in *it*-clefts and *have*-existentials are 'pseudo-relatives' (external to the DP they are interpreted with) seems well-motivated. Unfortunately, there is no evidence I am aware of, independent of the parenthetical insertion and extraction facts which McCawley presents, to indicate that predicate nominals or the noun phrase complement of *know* also support the pseudo-relative structure.

3.2.2. Subject Contact Clauses as Pseudo-relatives

If the proposal that subject contact clauses are simply unambiguous pseudo-relatives is correct, then they should display the same syntactic properties as pseudo-relatives, i.e. there should be evidence that they do not form a complex DP with the noun phrase that precedes them. This is borne out:

First, it appears that parenthetical insertion between the modified noun phrase and the relative clause is grammatical, as illustrated below.

(63)a. There's many a man, as you know, can't make a living these days.
b. I have a friend, incidentally, knows how to do that.
c. It was Bill, by the way, was responsible for that.
d. I knew a man there, incidentally, was a good friend of your father's.

There are also examples from written dialog:

(64)a. Is it our little omniomni you're trying to abuse? said Camier. You should know better. 'Tis he on the contrary fucks thee. Omniomni, the all-unfuckable. (MC26)

b. There's a couple above, said George, showed up there a short time back. (MC54)

This property apparently distinguishes subject from object contact clauses, which do not allow similar configurations:

(65)a. *There's many a man, as you know, John doesn't like.
b. *I have a friend, incidentally, John gets along with.
c. *It was Bill, by the way, John met.
d. *I knew a man there, incidentally, your father worked with.

However, this apparent contrast will be reconsidered presently.

Finally, subject contact clauses also permit counterexamples to the relative clause subcase of the complex noun phrase constraint. The extraction facts which McCawley presents are admittedly murky. However, the same level of murkiness is displayed by extraction from subject contact clauses:

(66)a. ?What things do you think there's nobody can fix t ?
b. ?What language do you have many students know well t ?
c. ?Which man do you think it was Bill was arguing with t ?
d. Which computer is Bill the only one can fix t?
e. ?Which guy do you know someone can't stand t ?

As with extraction from pseudo-relatives, these extractions do not have the characteristically severe level of ungrammaticality associated with CNPC violations:

(67) *Which book did you read the review that Mary wrote of t ?

Therefore, at least in the majority dialect, subject contact clauses seem to be licensed in all and only the environments in which pseudo-relatives appear and have all the syntactic properties of pseudo-relatives, as defined by McCawley. However, this in itself does not distinguish subject contact clauses from other relative clauses: all that has been established is that subject contact clauses pattern like other restrictive relatives in appearing external to the modified noun phrase in certain predicative constructions such as existentials. In the following section, some positive evidence will be presented that subject contact clauses are structurally identical to other contact clauses.

As a final point, note that the appearance of contact clauses in the coda of existentials may provide some insight into the syntax of existential sentences: in that whatever their internal structure, it must be the case (under the present analysis) that the binding relation between the postcopular noun phrase and a contact clause in the coda position can be maintained. This is possible if the postcopular DP c-commands the coda XP, as is the case in the 'small clause' analysis of existentials proposed by Stowell 1978, Safir 1982:

(68)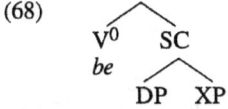

Nothing obviously excludes binding from the DP to the gap of a contact clause in the XP coda position.[32]

However, McNally 1992 provides convincing arguments against the small clause analysis of the post-copular material in existentials. Specifically, she argues on semantic grounds (McNally 1992: 13-15) that (i) the small clause analysis incorrectly predicts that other small clause constructions have existential-like counterparts, a prediction which is false and (ii) that the small clause analysis cannot simultaneously account for the definiteness effect and the predicate restriction. Finally, based on the difficulty of extraction from the coda, McNally proposes that the coda must be a non-selected adjunct, rather than a selected complement, as the small clause analysis entails. The following structure is proposed, where the XP coda is a V´-adjunct:

(69)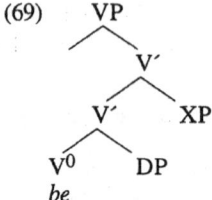

However, this structure is incompatible with the proposed analysis of contact clauses. In particular, the post-copular DP does not c-command the coda. Therefore, it would be unexpected that a syntactic A´-binding relation could hold between the DP and a variable within an IP in coda position.

Although McNally provides strong evidence that the predicate XP is a non-selected adjunct rather than a selected complement, there is no positive evidence (that I am aware of) to support the structure in (69) over a structure such as the following where the coda XP is adjoined to the post-copular DP:

(70)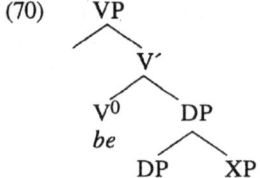

As the postcopular DP c-commands XP in this structure, it can bind an element within XP.[33] Furthermore, as this DP is shielded from direct association with other expressions by the mother DP, classifying it as an A´-position seems possible, as discussed in 2.2.2 above.[34] There may, in fact, be positive evidence in favor of this structure over that in (69): reciprocals and reflexives in expressions which are clearly DP-external codas can find their antecedents within the post-nominal DP:

(71)a. There was only Hume and Adams willing to talk to each other.
   b. There were two people in the class yesterday proud of themselves.

Therefore, I conclude that the claim that contact clauses can appear as DP-external modifiers in existentials is not inconsistent with the claim that an obligatory A´-binding relation holds between the relative head and the gap in the relative clause.

To conclude, it has been shown that subject contact clauses behave like other relative modifiers in that they appear as DP-external adjuncts in existentials and other predicative phrases. However, this fact does not in itself prove that subject contact clauses are a distinct construction from other contact clauses. In the following section, I show that there is much positive evidence to suggest that subject contact clauses are the same syntactic entity as object contact clauses.

3.3. Subject Contact Clauses are Relative Clauses

There is strong evidence that subject contact clauses are every bit as 'tightly connected' to the noun phrase they modify as other contact clause modifiers: i.e. they cannot stack, nor can they be extraposed. Note that although the examples containing stacked *wh*-relatives, (72)a and (73)a below, are grammatical, the corresponding examples with subject contact clauses are not. We can conclude, therefore, that at most one subject contact clause is permitted in predicate nominal constructions.

- (72)a. Bill is the only one who knows her well who can take that evening off.
- b. *Bill is the only one knows Mary well can take that evening off.

- (73)a. I knew a man who used to live down the street who spoke Irish.
- b. *I knew a man used to live down the street spoke Irish.

Note that only one XP is permitted in the predicate nominal construction:

(74) Bill is [$_{DP}$ the only one except Chuck] [$_{XP}$ free to take the evening off] [$_{XP}$*willing to go to that movie].

The relative grammaticality of (72)a and (73)a then must follow from the stacking of at least some of the relative clauses within the postcopular DP. Evidently, this option is not available with the subject contact clause examples, given the ungrammaticality of (72)b and (73)b. All other things being equal, it would seem reasonable to maintain that contact clauses do not stack.

However, existential sentences complicate matters somewhat, in that two (but at most two) subject contact clauses are permitted. Three full CP-relatives are fine, however:[35]

(75)a. There's this man lives across the street works in Dublin
   b. *There's this man lives across the street works in Dublin knows John.
   c. There's this man that lives across the street that works in Dublin that knows John.

However, I propose that the structure in (75)a is not a stacked structure and that the generalization that contact clauses cannot stack holds. Note that in existential constructions, it seems that at most one relative clause can appear in the XP position:

(76)a. There's [$_{DP}$ just John] [$_{XP}$ who's interested in seeing that movie] [$_{XP}$ *who can take the night off].

   b. There's [$_{DP}$ just you besides Chuck] [$_{XP}$ who's interested in seeing that movie][$_{XP}$ *who can go out tonight].

The relative grammaticality of (75)c must follow from the stacking of one or more relative clauses in the post-copular DP. Again, this option is evidently not available for subject contact clauses and therefore only two are ever permitted in the existential: one presumably internal to the postcopular DP and one in the XP-position, as indicated below:

(77) There's [$_{DP}$ a man lives next door][$_{XP}$ works in Dublin.]

Therefore, it seems reasonable to conclude that subject contact clauses cannot stack in general.

If subject contact clauses are structurally identical to object contact clauses it would be expected that they do not permit extraposition. Unfortunately, however, none of the environments in which subject contact clauses appear (in the majority dialect) allow 'extraposition from NP' very easily. The point can be made, however, using the more dialectal licensing of the construction in noun phrases headed by *any* and *every*:

(78)a. Anybody (who) can help out afterwards is welcome.
   b. Anybody is welcome *(who) can help out afterwards.

(79)a. Everybody (who) lives in the mountains has an accent.
b. Everybody has an accent *(who) lives in the mountains.

Therefore, it seems reasonable to conclude that both subject and object contact clauses are subject to the same adjacency restrictions.[36]

As discussed in the previous section, there is an apparent divergence in behavior between subject and object contact clauses with respect to parenthetical insertion. However, I believe that these facts are ultimately inconclusive due to structural ambiguity: it impossible to discern (in the general case) whether the parenthetical is actually inserted between the matrix predicate and the clause, or whether it is inserted to the left of the embedded VP in examples such as (63) above, as illustrated schematically below:

(80)a. I have a friend, incidentally, [knows how to do that.]
b. I have a friend [incidentally, knows how to do that.]

Some parentheticals, (e.g. *by the way*) prefer to appear between the relative head and the relative clause:

(81)a. It was Bill, by the way, who did it.
b. ?It was Bill who, by the way, did it.

Therefore, these parentheticals should serve to disambiguate the structures in (80) above: if subject contact clauses do permit parenthetical insertion between the modified head and modifier clause, then the result should be perfect; if subject contact clauses do not permit such configurations, then the result should be comparable to (81)b above. As the following examples indicate, the latter result obtains:

(82) ?It was Bill, by the way, did it.

Judgements are admittedly delicate. However, at the very least, there is no conclusive evidence that subject contact clauses differ from object contact clauses in allowing parenthetical insertion. On the contrary, there seems to be some evidence that both types of contact clause behave similarly in this respect.

If subject contact clauses are structurally identical to object contact clauses then it would also be expected that they reject adverbial adjunction to the left of the clause. This point is difficult to establish in that, as with parentheticals, it is difficult to discern for most adverbs whether they are adjoined to the clause-level or to VP, to the right of the subject position:

(83)a. Here's a problem [RC clearly [RC has a solution]].

b. Here's a problem [RC [VP clearly [VP has a solution]]].

However, there are some types of adverbs (locatives and bare-NP adverbs) which prefer sentence-initial position to VP-adjunct position:

(84)a. ??He last night went home.
b. Last night he went home.
c. He went home last night.

(85)a. ??the man who John last night met
b. the man who last night John met
c. the man who John met last night

(86)a. ??He at the pot-luck got really drunk.
b. At the pot-luck, he got really drunk.
c. He got really drunk at the pot-luck.

(87)a. ??the guy who Mary at the pot-luck argued with
b. the guy who at the pot-luck Mary argued with
c. the guy who Mary argued with at the pot-luck

The following examples suggest that adjunction to the left-edge of a subject contact clause is ungrammatical:

(88)a. That's the girl *(who) just yesterday was talking about you.
b. John is the guy *(who) at the pot-luck got really drunk.
c. It was Mary *(who) this morning got drunk.

Therefore, there is some evidence that, similar to object contact clauses, subject contact clauses lack a CP-level and are simply bare IPs.

If this proposal is correct, it should follow that those adverbs which only appear in VP-adjunct position should be fully grammatical in subject contact clauses. Jackendoff (1977: 51) points out that *hardly, merely, truly, simply* and *scarcely* are of this type:

(89)a. Albert is {hardly ... } being a fool.
b. *{Hardly ... } Albert is being a fool.
c. Albert is being a fool *{hardly ... }.

This prediction is borne out and the following examples are fully grammatical:

(90) a. That's something hardly gets mentioned these days.
   b. He's the one barely escaped with his life.
   c. Mary is the only one truly knows the language well.

Therefore, it seems clear that subject contact clauses do not differ from object contact clauses with respect to adverbial adjunction (*pace* Harris and Vincent 1980).[37]

Finally, it seems clear that subject contact clauses are restrictive modifiers: they clearly have the same semantic function as object contact clauses and other restrictive relatives: that of restrictive modification.

Given these syntactic and semantic similarities with object contact clauses, I propose that subject contact clauses are just that: contact clauses (IP-relatives) with a relativized subject position, as illustrated below.

(91)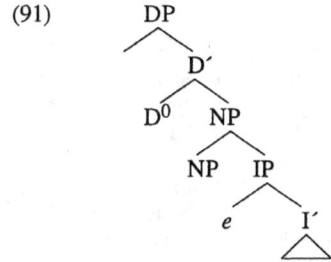

Significantly, if the empty category in the subject position is subject to the ECP, this analysis is incompatible with the account of the proper government requirements of subjects proposed in Rizzi 1990. Rizzi (1990: 32) adopts the conjunctive ECP, which requires that non-pronominal traces be properly head-governed (formally licensed) and antecedent-governed (identified):

(92) *(Conjunctive) ECP*:

   A non-pronominal empty category must be
   (i) properly head-governed
   (ii) θ-governed or antecedent governed.

Furthermore, Rizzi proposes (1990: 31) that proper head-government consists of head-government under strict c-command. This proposal entails that the only available head-governor for a subject trace is the complementizer, C^0.[38] In the proposed structure for subject contact clauses, therefore, there is no head-governor for the empty category and under Rizzi's proposals, the structure should be excluded.

However, there are several alternative possibilities which may render this proposal compatible with Rizzi's system: (i) only the trace of movement is subject to the ECP. Therefore, as contact clauses do not involve syntactic movement, the base-generated variable in this construction does not require proper-government; (ii) the empty category in contact clauses is pronominal (*pro*) and therefore exempt from ECP requirements, as I proposed in Doherty 1993; (iii) more radically, it could be claimed that this construction simply lacks an empty category altogether, and is simply a 'tensed VP'. However, there are two major empirical problems for such a proposal. First, these structures can be negated, showing that they are truly clausal:

(93)a. There's a man here can't speak English.
   b. Bill is the one wouldn't leave us alone.

Second, assuming that adjunction to the maximal projection of a relative modifier is excluded (as discussed in section 2). It would be expected that the adverbs which only adjoin to the VP-level should not be licit in subject contact clauses. However, this is not the case, as illustrated in the examples in (90) above.[39]

Therefore, I conclude that the structure of subject contact clauses is as in (91) above and that either the empty category is exempt from ECP requirements because it is base-generated or because it is a pronominal variable.

This conclusion leaves two issues unresolved, however. First there is the question of the distribution of subject contact clauses: why should subject but not object contact clauses be subject to these distributional constraints? Secondly, the behavior of subject contact clauses diverges from object contact clauses in co-ordination structures: only the latter co-ordinates easily with full CP restrictive relatives:

(94)a. This is the man John met and that Mary likes.
   b. This is the man John met and who Mary likes.

Subject contact clauses are associated with a certain degree of uneasiness in such structures. Judgements seem variable, however:

(95)a. There's plenty have more need ?(and who aren't getting it).
   b. John is the only one can do the job ??(and that lives nearby).
   c. I have an idea might work *?(and that could just save the day).

I argue in the following sections that these properties may follow from the proposed classification of contact clauses as postnominal modifiers. First, however, I wish to point out that the distribution of subject contact clauses for many speakers is much wider than has been traditionally observed. In particular, the construction appears in many contexts from which McCawley's class of pseudo-relatives are excluded, which is recalcitrant for the claim that subject contact clauses are simply a syntactic encoding of the pseudo-relative construction.

3.4. Distribution: Liberal Dialects

The distribution of subject contact clauses in many dialects (e.g. Appalachian English, Hiberno-English) seems much wider than has been traditionally observed. In addition to the core environments outlined in the previous sections, the construction appears in noun phrases headed by a universal quantifier:[40]

(96) a. She ... gave me all the change was in the house. (GF150)
 b. Everyone lives in the mountains has an accent all to theirself. (W1)
 c. Every one of my children went to that school, they spelled their names wrong.

Noun phrases headed by 'free-choice' *any* also license the construction:[41]

(97) a. Any man can't fight for his friends had better be dead. (C326)
 b. Anyone sees you with that hole in your sweater will think you're broke.
 c. Anybody came into the town had to leave their cars and walk up.

In Hiberno-English at least, the construction is also licensed in intensional contexts:

(98) a. I'd like to meet the man would play-act on Larry. (GF48)
 b. You're like a man was up all night. (GF88)
 c. I'm looking for someone speaks Irish well.

It also appears more frequently in predicate nominals:

(99) a. It was a thing came naturally to my mind. (LN141)
   b. They're the kind of people would do that.
   c. The bad story is the quickest goes round. (GF150)
   d. That was the stormiest night ever was in this parish. (LN12)
   e. They say Micheál Mór was a man always paid his dues well. (LN98)

However, it is not the case that the construction is licensed generally in predicate nominals. There are many predicate nominals which reject modification by subject contact clauses. Note the ungrammaticality of examples such as the following:

(100) *John is a doctor treats his patients well.

These examples of subject contact clauses are unlike those licensed in existentials and clefts in that they are internal to the noun phrase they modify. It is clear that they form a complex noun phrase with the relative head. First, note that those examples headed by quantifiers (including 'free-choice' *any*) can appear in a canonical noun phrase position: i.e. subject position (e.g. (96)b,c and (97) above). Secondly, note that parenthetical insertion is not permitted in any of these environments:

(101) a. *She gave me all the change, as you know, was in the house.
   b. *Everyone, incidentally, lives in the mountains has an accent all to themselves.

(102) a. *We need someone, as you know, can do the job right.
   b. *I'd like to meet the man, by the way, could beat Larry.

(103) a. *The bad story is the quickest, incidentally, goes around.
   b. *John was a man, as you know, always paid his dues well.

It seems reasonable to conclude that the contact clause modifier is internal to DP in these examples. That is, in these dialects, the licensing domain for the pseudo-relative structure and the licensing domain for subject contact clauses are not co-extensive. It is clear however, that these instances of subject contact clauses are subject to the same syntactic constraints as other contact clauses noted above: (i) they cannot undergo extraposition, as indicated in (78-9) above; (ii) in addition, they cannot stack:

(104)a. Everyone lives here (*knows Mary) says she's nice.
b. We need someone lives nearby (*speaks Irish).
c. Michael is a man always pays his debts (*is always punctual).

Furthermore, they show the same uneasiness in co-ordinating with full CP-relative clauses:

(105)a. Anyone would do that ?(and that wouldn't even apologize afterwards) should be put in jail.
b. Everybody lives in this area ??(and that knows him well) says he is a nice man.
c. You look like a man was up all night ?(and that just saw a ghost).
d. You're not the first challenged him ?(and that lived to tell the tale).

Therefore, I conclude that these instances of subject contact clauses differ from those presented in previous sections only in that they are DP-internal modifiers. This result casts further doubt on the claim that subject contact clauses are unambiguously pseudo-relatives.

3.5. Summary

In sum, subject contact clauses are non-distinct from object contact clauses in syntactic properties and in semantic interpretation (*pace* Erdmann 1980, McCawley 1981, 1988 and Henry 1995).[42] In some dialects, they also appear with object contact clauses and other relative clauses as DP-internal modifiers. However, they diverge in behavior in two major ways: (i) they are subject to a series of distributional constraints; (ii) they do not co-ordinate freely with other restrictive relatives. In the following section, I claim that these properties are not unique to subject contact clauses at all but are typical of many other postnominal modifiers. First, however, some previous proposals are examined.

4. EXPLAINING THE DISTRIBUTION OF SUBJECT CONTACT CLAUSES

Some previous studies claim that the distribution of subject contact clauses is determined by pragmatic or semantic factors. These are discussed below.

4.1. Previous Accounts

4.1.1. Pragmatic Accounts

Based on the fact that subject contact clauses appear most frequently in existentials and clefts, various works suggest that the factor determining the distribution of the construction is discourse-oriented, e.g. Erdmann 1980 claims that subject contact clauses are limited to focus-constructions. An essentially similar proposal is advanced in Prince 1981 who suggests that subject contact clauses are used to keep strongly novel or informative material out of subject position (Prince 1981: 247):

> "Anthony Kroch (personal communication) has noted that in his large corpus of oral discourse, ALL instances of subject relative marker deletion occur in sentences ... where the syntactically main clause is informationally weak ... and the subordinate clause is highly informative. Thus it seems that the more formal counterparts to (106) are not (107), as one might think, but (109):[my numbering]"

(106) a. We got a lot of fancy Cadillac cars don't tip.
 b. I had a great-great-great-grandfather or something fought that Revolution.
 c. There was a piece of four-inch bone never mended.

(107) a. We have a lot of fancy Cadillac cars which/that don't tip.
 b. I had a great-great-great-grandfather or something who/that fought that Revolution.
 c. There was a piece of four-inch bone which/that never mended.

(108) a. A lot of fancy Cadillac cars don't tip.
 b. A great-great-great-grandfather or something fought that Revolution.
 c. A piece of four-inch bone never mended.

The discourse-theoretic approach is initially promising and provides a straightforward explanation of the exclusion of the construction from environments such as (45) above, repeated below:

(109) a. *The man worked there was a friend of mine.
 b. *I gave a ticket to a man comes every day.

However, these approaches face some problems. In particular, the fact that subject contact clauses occasionally do appear in subject position, as illustrated below, seems recalcitrant for Prince's proposal in particular.

(110) a. John is the only one can do it.
b. The only one can do it is John.

Furthermore, the fact that for many speakers, the construction is licensed in environments which are not obviously associated with any degree of novelty or focus (e.g. in noun phrases headed by universal quantifiers) is also problematic.

4.1.2. Non-Referentiality

In previous work, (Doherty 1993), I argued that the distribution of subject contact clauses is semantically determined. Specifically, it was proposed that IP-relatives with subject gaps are licensed just in case the noun phrase they modify is 'non-referential' in the pretheoretical sense that it fails to denote an individual in the real world (an extensional individual). This constraint serves to exclude the construction from extensional contexts such as the following:[43]

(111) a. *A man speaks Irish walked into the bar.
b. ??I gave a lift to this man knows Mary.

Adopting the proposal of McNally 1992 that postcopular noun phrases do not denote individuals in the real world (she specifically proposes that they denote 'nominalized functions'), then the licensing of subject contact clauses in existential and copular sentences may also fall under this generalization.

This approach also covers the licensing of the construction in intensional contexts, and also predicts the strongly preferred if not obligatory *de dicto* reading of noun phrases modified by subject contact clauses in opaque contexts:

(112) a. We want someone that knows John. (*de dicto* & *de re*)
b. We want someone knows John. (*de dicto*)

Finally, assuming that material in the restriction of a quantifier is non-extensional in the required sense, this claim is consistent with the appearance of subject contact clauses in noun phrases headed by universal quantifiers, as the relative clause ends up in the restriction on the quantifier:

(113)a. Everybody lives in the mountains has an accent.
   b. $\forall x$: live-in-the-mountains(x) [has-an-accent(x)]

However, there are a number of problems with this semantic generalization: (i) it is not obviously compatible with the licensing of subject contact clauses in the complement of *know*:

(114) I knew a man owned twenty restaurants.

It is not clear that a non-referential semantics is available for the object of *know* in such sentences; (ii) it predicts that *all* predicate nominals license subject contact clauses, which has been shown in 3.4 above not to be the case; (iii) it predicts that *all* quantifiers license the construction. This prediction is false, however. Many quantificational determiners are incompatible with subject contact clauses:[44]

(115)a. *?A few people speak Irish live in this parish still.
   b. *?Many people speak Irish live in this parish still.

Finally, the generalization is simply too strong in that if something as 'deep' as non-referentiality is the sole licensing factor for subject contact clauses, then little if any variation among speakers or dialects is predicted to occur. As it stands, the generalization (partially) covers only the most liberal dialect.

4.2. The Distribution of Post-Nominal Modifiers

Although I cannot provide an explicit analysis of the distribution of subject contact clauses here, I show that the distributional constraints described in the previous sections are not unique to this construction. Other post-nominal modifiers, which in the earliest generative analyses were viewed as 'reduced relatives' (Smith 1964) are also subject to similar if not identical distributional constraints.[45]

Consider that adjectival predicates (*eager to help, ready to help*) are excluded to varying degrees from 'extensional contexts', as are subject contact clauses:

(116)a. *I was very grateful to a certain man aware of our difficulties.
   b. *?I gave a grammar to a student eager to learn.
   c. *A man proud of his daughter congratulated her at the party.
   d. ??A friend able to help came over last night

These modifiers are also sensitive to the determiner of the noun phrase they modify, as are subject contact clauses. The definite determiner in general is much less acceptable than the indefinite:

(117) a. ??A man speaks Irish was at the party.
b. *The man speaks Irish was at the party.

c. ??A friend able to help came over last night
d. *The friend aware of our difficulties called.

In addition, these predicates show similar interactions with quantificational determiners as subject contact clauses. They are generally grammatical with universal quantifiers but show varying degrees of acceptability with others:

(118) a. Anybody aware of this problem was at the meeting.
b. Everybody aware of this problem was at the meeting.
c. ??Few people aware of this problem were at the meeting.
d. ?Many people aware of this problem were at the meeting.
e. ?Some people aware of this problem were at the meeting.
f. ??No-one aware of this problem was at the meeting.

Furthermore, as with subject contact clauses, these modifiers are generally acceptable in existentials and other copular sentences:[46]

(119) a. There is no-body here (*aware of our difficulties*, etc.)
b. John is the only one (*aware of our difficulties*, etc.)
c. I knew no-one (*aware of our difficulties*, etc.)

They also appear happily as modifiers to noun phrases in intensional contexts, where they seem to admit only a *de dicto* reading of the modified noun phrase.

(120) a. I'd like to find a person (*aware of our difficulties* ...)
b. I'm looking for a person (*eager to learn* etc.)
c. I'm looking for someone (*able to help* ...)

Furthermore, many postnominal modifiers show similar distributional constraints to subject contact clauses in predicate nominals. Recall that even the most liberal dialects do not license subject contact clauses generally in predicate nominals. The following represent the best and worst cases:

(121) a. *John is a doctor treats his patients well.
   b. John is the only one can do it.
   c. ?John is a man always pays his debts.
   d. That's the one wants to see you.

Similar restrictions obtain with post-nominal modifiers such as *able to help* and *eager to finish, ready to quit*:

(122) a. ?*John is a doctor (*ready to quit* etc.)
   b. John was the only one (*able to help* etc.)
   c. ?John is a man (*eager to finish* etc.)
   d. That's the one (*ready to quit* etc.)

Furthermore, these expressions are similar to subject contact clauses in that they display difficulty in co-ordinating with full CP-relatives:

(123) a. Anybody able to help ??(and that would refuse her) should be shot.
   b. Everybody eager to leave ?(and who had the means to) left town before the predicted earthquake.
   c. We need someone eager to learn ?(and who speaks French).

Therefore, in conclusion, the constraints on the distribution of subject contact clauses are not unique to the construction at all but are typical of many postnominal modifiers. This conclusion raises two questions (at least): (i) what accounts for these restrictions?; (ii) what accounts for the divergence in behavior between subject and object contact clauses?

I do not attempt to provide an answer to the first question here. However, the proposed analysis of contact clauses may provide the beginnings of an answer to the second. Under the IP-hypothesis, contact clauses are classified among the set of postnominal modifiers in that both constructions involve direct identification of their missing subject with the denotation of the modified noun phrase. The divergence in behavior between subject and object contact clauses may lie in the fact that the former involves identification of the modified noun phrase with the missing subject and the latter does not: i.e. these distributional constraints are a feature of postnominal modifiers with 'subject gaps.'

Not all postnominal modifiers which appear to have a missing subject display these constraints. For example, many passive participles do not seem to be subject to similar restrictions:[47]

(124)a. The man arrested for murder escaped this morning.
   b. The police found the man murdered by a gunman in an alleyway.

Furthermore, some postnominal modifiers which have a 'subject gap' (e.g. present participles such as *willing to help*) behave distributionally like the modifiers in (124) above.

In sum, the classification of contact clauses as postnominal modifiers involving direct identification of the denotation of the modified noun phrase with an argument of the modifier is consistent with the distributional constraints on subject-gap contact relatives. As pointed out above, many postnominal modifiers with unsaturated external arguments (though admittedly not all) are subject to very similar, if not identical, constraints.

5. CHAPTER SUMMARY

In conclusion, this chapter presents empirical evidence for the IP-hypothesis of the structure of *that*-less relatives (contact clauses). The conclusion that these relative clauses are simply IPs is perhaps initially surprising. However, it was demonstrated that this proposal is consistent with current understanding of the syntax and semantics of relative clauses. Assuming that the relative head is an A´-position which directly binds the gap in the IP-relative, the basic interpretive and syntactic similarities between contact clauses and (full) relative clauses can be accounted for.

The analysis also has a number of other pleasing consequences. In particular, the proposal that these clauses lack operator movement provides the basis for a plausible account of the adjacency condition which these clauses are subject to: IP is licensed as a relative clause just in case the variable position is A´-bound by the relative head. Therefore, if the integrity of this binding relation is destroyed, such as in extraposed or stacked structures, IP cannot function as a relative clause modifier.

Finally, novel evidence was provided for the relative clause status of subject contact clauses and it was determined that their distributional constraints are not peculiar to the construction but are typical of many other postnominal modifiers with subject gaps.

NOTES

1. Throughout this chapter data from written sources is occasionally presented. Where this is the case, the source is given in an

abbreviated form. These abbreviations have the following interpretations:

C	Curme 1931.
GF	*The Green Fool.* Patrick Kavanagh. Penguin. 1971.
E	Erdmann 1980.
LN	*The Last of the Name.* Charles McGlinchy, edited by Brian Friel. Belfast and Wolfboro, New Hampshire: Blackstaff Press. 1986
MC	*Mercier and Camier.* Samuel Beckett. Picador. 1988.
Q	Quirk *et al.* 1972
U	*Ulysses.* James Joyce. corrected text edition. Penguin. 1988.
W	Wolfram and Christian 1976.
WD	*Winter of Our Discontent.* John Steinbeck. New York: Viking Press. 1961.

2. In the analysis of Chomsky and Lasnik 1977 a rule of 'deletion in Comp' optionally deletes the complementizer *that* or the relative pronoun (*ibid* 435). At least one must be null in order to avoid a violation of the 'Doubly Filled Comp' filter.
3. Weisler 1980 also argues (specifically from extraposition facts) that contact clauses are bare S (IP) relative clause modifiers.
4. There appears to be some variation among speakers in the acceptability of stacked structures. (Stockwell *et al.* 1973: 442-47).
5. These examples are adapted from Weisler (1980: 626).
6. An alternative explanation of the exclusion of pied-piping is available under the assumption that null operators are morphologically [-*wh*]: i.e. unlike overt *wh*-operators, they do not permit an expression within which they are embedded (such as a PP) to function as a syntactic operator. See 2.2.1. below.
7. Furthermore, it will be shown in section two below that there is strong evidence for the presence of a syntactic A´-chain in contact clauses.
8. Strictly speaking, relative clauses denote sets of individuals under the standard Montagovian analysis which gives them the translation in (18)b.
9. The adoption of the DP-hypothesis of noun phrase structure (Abney 1987) makes available two possible adjunction sites for the relative clause: NP-adjunct position, or DP-adjunct position. I have chosen the former. Nothing in the present discussion hinges on this. However, the possibility of adjunction to the DP-level becomes important in the discussion of existential sentences in 3.2.2 below.
10. I illustrate the Subjacency effects with the noun complement subcase of the Complex Noun Phrase Constraint.

11. This phrase could perhaps be identified with the lower CP of 'recursive CP' structures (in the sense of Rizzi and Roberts 1989, Vikner 1991, 1996, McCloskey 1992 and others) or the 'PolarityP' of Culicover 1991.
12. See section 5 of Chapter 2 for references and further discussion of these issues.
13. Bošković (1997: 25f.) also proposes, from purely theoretical motivation, that contact relatives are IPs but adopts the operator-movement analysis considered in (29)a. As pointed out above, however, it is not obvious how such an analysis can be reconciled with the adverbial adjunction facts discussed here.
14. Under the assumption that relative clauses adjoin to DP rather than NP the relative head can still be classified as an A´-position (see Bianchi 1991 who argues that the relative head in Italian infinitival relatives, which she assumes are adjoined to DP, is also an A´-position).
15. In earlier work (Doherty 1993) I argued that this variable should be analyzed as a null pronominal variable, *pro*, following the proposal of Cinque 1990 that a subclass of *wh*-constructions (e.g. parasitic gaps) should be analyzed as null resumptive pronoun strategies. Such a proposal is consistent with the failure of pied-piping in contact clauses: *pro* is by definition exclusively nominal. However, this proposal suffers from a drawback in that overt resumptive pronouns are not equivalently grammatical in contact clauses:

    *the man you saw him

    It is not entirely clear how to exclude overt resumptives from this structure if null resumptives are admitted. However, see Doherty 1993 for some possibilities. See also Goodluck 1997.
16. Reinhart 1980 argues that extraposed relative clauses are adjoined at the sentence-level, rather than to VP.
17. It might perhaps be objected that the binding relation could be restored at LF under Reconstruction. However, recall from 2.2 above that the empty category in contact clauses is essentially non-distinct from the trace of *wh*-movement. One of the characteristics of trace is that it is subject to the Proper Binding Condition: i.e. trace must be bound (Saito 1992: 80, citing Fiengo 1977, Chomsky 1986b among others). Therefore, given the other similarities between the empty category of contact clauses and *wh*-trace, it would be unexpected if it were exempt from the Proper Binding Condition and could remain unbound.
18. That is, if c-command is interpreted as the following relation:

α c-commands β, iff. every branching node dominating α also dominates β.

19. I assume here that even if the index of the relative head is present on each node of the adjunction structure in (33), these segments cannot count as autonomous binding operators.
20. See section 5 of Chapter 2 for further discussion and references on this issue.
21. This is Jespersen's (1909-49) term. The construction has gone by a variety of other names in the traditional literature e.g. 'asyndetic relative clause' (Curme 1931) or the 'zero or απο κοινου construction' (Visser 1963). I here follow Jespersen's terminology which seems the most transparent.
22. Unless otherwise indicated, all data is from Hiberno-English.
23. This example is attributed to Wilson Gray. Chomsky and Lasnik conclude on this basis that the proposed 'NP *Tns* VP' Filter (*[$_{NP}$ tense VP]) cannot apply universally.
24. Furthermore, sentence-initial examples are much more frequent in dialects which license subject contact clauses more liberally:

> (i) Everybody lives in the mountains has an accent. (W1)

In addition, Bever and Langendoen (1970: 441n.10) also note the following examples:

> (ii) A lad would kill his father, I'm thinking, would face a foxy devil with a pitchpike.
> (iii) Anybody knows Harry'd say the same.

25. Jespersen (1909-49: 152) dissents from this position, however:

"we may ... say that though there is no connecting word, the two parts of the sentence are more intimately joined together than when the relative pronouns *who* or *which* are used ... Before contact clauses we never have a pause; the intonation too, of the whole sentence, the clause included, shows unity and is different from that of two independent sentences."

26. This term should not be confused with the Romance 'pseudo-relative' construction discussed in the work of Cinque, Guasti and others.
27. The examples in (51) and (52) are McCawley's. Chung and McCloskey 1983 also provide many examples of this type.
28. McNally also provides strong arguments against a possible analysis of the predicate XP as an IP-adjunct. However, rather than labor the point further here, I refer the reader to McNally's discussion (1992: 44-6).

29. The examples in this discussion are McNally's: (56) and (57) are McNally's (89) and (90).
30. This is McNally's (92). The observation is attributed to Ladusaw 1979.
31. McNally also provides convincing evidence against the specific arguments of Williams 1984 in favor of a complex DP analysis. However, rather than present them here, I refer the reader to McNally 1992 for discussion.
32. It is a question, however, to what extent this can be regarded as A´-binding, given that the DP resides in the subject of a small clause which is standardly assumed to be an A-position.
33. One possible objection to this analysis is that, at first blush, it appears to involve adjunction to an argument (the postcopular noun phrase), in violation of the Adjunction Prohibition discussed extensively in Chapter 2. However, there is good reason to believe that the predicate of the copula cannot be an argument in any real sense. For example, if this were the case, then predicational copular sentences should uniformly give rise to Condition C effects:

   He is a doctor.

   Rather, the predicate of the copula seems to assign, rather than receive a θ–role. Thanks to Sandy Chung for discussion about this issue.
34. Thanks to Louise McNally for useful discussion about these issues.
35. Lodge 1979 also makes the observation that two subject contact clauses can appear in the existential construction.
36. This analysis predicts that two but only two object contact clauses should appear in existential constructions also. However, for reasons unclear to me, it is difficult to admit more than two relative clauses with an object gap in existentials:

    (i) There was somebody that I met yesterday that Mary knows.
    (ii) #There was somebody that I met yesterday that Mary likes that John works with.

   However, the degree of ungrammaticality displayed by the corresponding contact clause form of (ii) is much greater:

    (iii) *There was somebody I met yesterday Mary likes John works with.

   Therefore, it seems reasonable to conclude that object contact clauses also display the constraint that two but at most two can appear in existentials.

37. Harris and Vincent 1980 argue that subject contact clauses admit averbial adjunction, based on the grammaticality of examples such as the following:

   (i) It was John actually did it.
   (ii) There's a woman urgently wants to see you.

   The adverbs *actually* and *urgently* adjoin to VP, in addition to IP, however:

   (iii) John actually did it.
   (iv) A woman urgently wants to see you.

   Examples such as (i) and (ii), therefore, receive an alternative explanation as instances of adverbial adjunction to VP.
38. See Chapter 4 for a fuller discussion of these issues.
39. Furthermore, assuming that modals are lexical I^0, the examples in (93) provide further evidence that these constructions contain an inflectional projection.
40. Example (96)b is from Appalachian English. The others are Hiberno-English.
41. However, this reduces to the quantificational case above, given the availability of a universal quantifier analysis of 'free-choice' *any* (e.g. Carlson 1981).
42. Based on some of the distributional restrictions discussed above, Henry (1995: 130f.) argues that subject contact clauses cannot be restrictive relative structures. Instead, she proposes that they instantiate a kind of overtly introduced Topic-Comment structure in which the modified nominal is a Topic and the clausal element a Comment, essentially a matrix rather than an embedded clause:

   (i) There's [$_{Topic}$ a man] [$_{Comment}$ ∅ wants to see you.]

   This approach is attractive, it is claimed, as it provides the basis for an explanation of the distribution of these clauses: many of the environments in which subject contact clauses appear involve the introduction of a new topic into the discourse (Henry 1995: 132). However, regardless of the accuracy of this claim, it seems untenable for purely syntactic reasons: there is strong evidence that subject contact clauses are embedded and not matrix clauses.

   First, recall from (96) and (97) above that subject contact clauses often appear within the subject noun phrase. It is not at all obvious how the subject contact clause in such examples could be analyzed as a matrix clause.

   Second, further evidence against this proposal is provided by existential sentences. Note that existentials may contain more than one relative clause:

(ii) There's a man who lives down the street who works in London.

It is striking that existentials may also contain more than one subject contact clause:

(iii) There's a man lives down the street works in London.

This fact points clearly to the embedded status of subject contact clauses. It is unclear how the Topic-Comment analysis could extend to such examples, given that each Topic-Comment structure contains at most one Topic and one Comment.

Finally, root and relative clauses cannot co-ordinate:

(vi) *John is a teacher and who knows French.

If subject contact clauses are matrix clauses, therefore, one would expect the same severe level of ungrammaticality to obtain when subject contact clauses are co-ordinated with full relative clauses. As is clear from (95) and (105) above, however, this is simply not the case.

In sum, the body of syntactic evidence pointing to the embedded nature of subject contact clauses is overwhelming. As a central assumption of the Topic-Comment analysis is that subject contact clauses are matrix and not embedded clauses, this approach seems unlikely to succeed.

43. In Doherty 1993, I argued that contact clauses are null resumptive pronoun strategies (following Cinque 1990 that A´-chains can terminate in the null pronominal *pro*). Noting that subject resumptive pronouns are excluded from most languages (e.g. Irish), I argued that the general ungrammaticality of subject contact clauses in English follows from this constraint (the Highest Subject Constraint). Adopting the analysis of this constraint of McCloskey 1990 as a Binding Theory violation, and furthermore assuming that only referential expressions bear indices visible to the Binding Theory, it is predicted that IP-relatives with a subject *pro* are licensed just in case the noun phrase they modify is non-referential.
44. This fact is discussed in more detail in the following section.
45. Thanks to James McCawley for suggesting that I take a look at reduced relatives.
46. The distribution of subject contact clauses and these other postnominal modifiers diverges in *It*-Clefts:

It was Bill *(who was) aware of the murder.

This construction admits only tensed clauses in the coda position.
47. Some passive participles do seem to show similar distributional constraints in that they are compatible with determiners such as *any* but not the definite determiner:

> (i) The horse *(that was) raced past the barn fell.
> (ii) Any horse (that was) raced past the barn fell.

The exclusion of (i) has been previously ascribed to parsing difficulties (see Bever and Langendoen (1971: 437f.) for some discussion and references). However, this seems questionable in the light of (ii) above, which seems acceptable for many speakers.

CHAPTER 4

Extraction Theory

1. INTRODUCTION

This chapter explores the consequences of the IP-hypothesis for the explanation of the '*that*-trace effect': i.e. the relative ungrammaticality of subject extraction across an overt complementizer in English:

(1)a. *Who$_i$ did Bill say that t_i left?
   b. Who$_i$ did Bill say t_i left?

This effect was first brought to light in the generative literature in Perlmutter 1971 and its proper explanation has been a point of much contention to date.

Under the CP-hypothesis, the analytical task involved in the explanation of the *that*-trace effect is considerable, given the grammaticality of subject extraction across null but not overt complementizers:

(2)a. *Who$_i$ do you say [$_{CP}$ [$_{C'}$ that [$_{IP}$ t_i left?]]]

   b. Who$_i$ do you say [$_{CP}$ [$_{C'}$ Ø [$_{IP}$ t_i left?]]]

This task is complicated by the apparent reversal of the pattern in relative clauses:

(3) the key [$_{CP}$ that [$_{C'}$ t opens the chest]]

Previous accounts analyze the effect as either a violation of Locality, broadly construed, (e.g. Pesetsky 1982a, Chomsky 1986a) where the complementizer blocks a requisite local relation between the moved element and the gap, or as a violation of the formal licensing condition on traces (head-government) (e.g. Aoun *et al.* 1987, Rizzi 1990). The IP-hypothesis has positive implications for these accounts and in particular, allows for a significant reduction in the complexity of the head-government account of Rizzi 1990.

The core of the head-government account is the assumption that complementizers are improper head-governors and so cannot license a subject trace, as in (2)a. This account entails that null complementizers, as in (2)b themselves count as proper governors. However, the question is: why should this be? The answer of Rizzi 1990 is that UG makes available a mechanism of 'agreement in comp' which permits complementizers to bear agreement features and so function as proper head-governors. In some languages, this agreement is morphologically visible such as the well-known *que/qui* alternation in French. However, in English, it is proposed, agreeing complementizers are morphologically null (in complement clauses at least). Various qualifications are required to account for the full range of data.

The IP-hypothesis allows for a considerable reduction in the complexity of the head-government account. For example, the problem of explaining why the null complementizer in (2)b is a proper governor does not arise, as there simply are no null complementizers in embedded declaratives. Therefore, no recourse to the mechanism of 'agreement in comp' is required in these cases. Furthermore, adopting an *in situ* analysis of local subject extraction (Chomsky 1986a, Grimshaw 1993), (4) below, the question of the proper government properties of null complementizers can be eliminated entirely:

(4)a. [$_{IP}$ Who [$_{I'}$ left?]]

b. I wonder [$_{IP}$ who [$_{I'}$ left?]]

Therefore, the complexity of the head government account can be maximally reduced.

The structure of this chapter is as follows. In section 2, the basic facts which an adequate analysis of the *that*-trace effect should take account of are outlined. In section 3, the previous accounts of the effect are discussed and in section 4 the implications of the IP-hypothesis for the head-government account are explored in detail.

2. THE *THAT*-TRACE EFFECT

Before exploring the consequences of IP-complementation for the analysis of the *that*-trace effect, I first want to outline the facts which an adequate analysis should take account of. First, there is the question of cross-linguistic variability: i.e. the fact that this effect obtains in some languages, such as English but not in others, such as Irish and Italian, which freely allow subject extraction across overt complementizers:

(5) Cé adeir sé a chonaic sé aréir? (Irish)
 who that.say he that saw he last night
 'Who does he say he saw last night?'

(6) Chi credi che abbia telefonato? (Italian)
 who believe.you that has telephoned
 'Who do you believe telephoned?'

There has been some debate in the literature as to the relevant parameters. For example, Perlmutter 1971 conjectures that the absence of *that*-trace effects is a property of languages which do not allow inflectional subjects (i.e. non-*pro*-drop languages). However, Perlmutter's conjecture has been called into doubt by work such as Maling and Zaenen 1978 who show that Icelandic and at least one 'dialect' of Dutch (neither of which allow inflectional subjects) also lack the *that*-trace effect. Van der Auwera 1984 also points out that this situation obtains in other languages such as Old English, Bavarian and Papiamentu.

Furthermore, there is variation within languages which have been claimed to display the *that*-trace effect. For example, *that*-trace violations are not particularly ungrammatical for many speakers of English.[1] This is confirmed by Sobin's 1987 study of college-age speakers of American English which reports that many subjects accepted *that*-trace configurations as fully grammatical. The situation seems comparable in other languages which have been claimed to display the *that*-trace effect. For example, Taraldsen (1980: 14) reports that Norwegian displays the effect on a par with English:

(7) *hvor mange mennesker tror du at vil komme?
 how many people believe you that will come
 'How many people do you believe will come?'

However, others report that some speakers of Norwegian accept *that*-trace configurations as grammatical, e.g. Peter Svenonius (p.c.), Van der Auwera (1984: 258):

(8) Den mannen som vi trodde at ville vinne
 the man that we believe that will win
 'the man that we believe that will win'

Therefore, whatever the ultimate analysis of the effect, it should be flexible enough to account for language-internal variation such as this.

While there is variation among speakers as to the grammaticality of *that*-trace configurations, there seems to be no such variation with other 'complementizer-trace' effects:[2]

(9)a. *Which man aren't you sure whether *t* left?
b. *Who do you wonder if *t* will be on time?

These examples are generally agreed to be much more strongly ungrammatical than the corresponding *that*-trace violations, a result which suggests that an additional or distinct constraint may be violated.

Finally, as noted in the introduction, the effect is apparently suspended in relative clauses:

(10) the man [CP that [IP *t* left]]

In sum, an adequate account should address a variety of related questions in addition to providing an explanation of the basic contrast in (1). In the following section, some previous accounts of the effect are reviewed concentrating primarily on the head-government account of Rizzi 1990.

3. PREVIOUS ACCOUNTS

The earliest accounts viewed the effect as resulting from a condition on the operation of transformations, such as the 'Fixed Subject Constraint' of Bresnan 1972[1979] or as a condition on the output of transformations, as in Perlmutter 1971 and Chomsky and Lasnik 1977, who propose a surface filter, the '*that*-trace' filter (Chomsky and Lasnik 1977: 451):

(11)   *[NP that [NP *e*]]

unless S´ or its trace are in the context [NP NP _].

Later work attempts to account for the effect by less stipulative means. For example, Pesetsky 1982a and Chomsky 1986a attempt to explain the effect as a violation of locality: the intervention of *that* between the subject trace and its antecedent destroys a requisite local relation between them.[3] More recent work ascribes the effect to a failure of the formal licensing requirement on traces, i.e. proper head-government.

3.1. Locality

3.1.1. Locality as Binding

Pesetsky 1982a (building in part on earlier work by Taraldsen 1980) argues that the Nominative Island Condition applies to the trace of NP-movement (Pesetsky 1982a: 300):

(12)   *Nominative Island Condition*

A nominative anaphor cannot be free in S´.

This binding principle ensures that anaphors must appear in the same clause as their antecedents and when extended to subject traces, it ensures that there must be an element in Comp coindexed with the subject trace.

Pesetsky adopts the 'Doubly-Filled Comp Filter' (Chomsky and Lasnik 1977) which demands that only one element appear in Comp, ensuring that *wh*-words cannot be followed by overt complementizers:

(13)a. *Who that came?
   b.   *the man who that came

He also adopts the rule of 'Free Deletion in Comp' (Chomsky and Lasnik 1977) which precedes the 'Doubly Filled Comp' filter. This rule allows for the free deletion of any element in Comp, deriving the alternation between *that* and ∅ in complement clauses. Pesetsky's innovation, however, is the extension of the rule to intermediate traces. That is, an intermediate trace can count as α in the following schema:

(14)   *[$_{COMP}$ α β]

Therefore, subject extraction from a complement clause has two possible outputs: either the complementizer deletes, as in (15)a or the trace deletes, as in (15)b:

(15)a. [$_{S´}$ [$_{COMP}$ t_i ∅] [$_S$ t $_{[NOM]i}$ …

   b.   *[$_{S´}$ [$_{COMP}$ ∅ that] [$_S$ t $_{[NOM]i}$ …

However, the deletion of the trace in (15)b leads to a violation of the NIC, as the subject trace is no longer bound in S´ and the *that*-trace effect is derived. Therefore, the central insight of this account is that complementizers cannot count as an appropriate antecedent for the subject trace.

In relative clauses, however, it must be the case that the complementizer does count as an appropriate antecedent for a subject trace. A re-indexing rule which transmits the index of the intermediate trace onto the complementizer is adopted (Pesetsky 1982a: 306):

(16) COMP Contraction

$[_{COMP} \text{WH}_i \text{ that }] \rightarrow [_{COMP} \text{ that}_i]$

This rule ensures that no NIC violation obtains in the case of *that*-relatives. Although this rule seems stipulative, as Pesetsky points out, it may have morphologically overt counterparts in other languages such as French:

(17) l'homme que tu crois (qui/*que) *t* viendra
 the.man that you believe that will.come
 'the man that you believe that will come'

In addition, the use of a morphologically distinct complementizer in relative clauses in many languages may also constitute an overt reflex of the operation of this rule, e.g. Norwegian obligatorily uses *som* in relative clauses, as opposed to the usual subordinating *at* complementizer, as illustrated below (Pesetsky 1982: 307).

(18) en Mann (som/*at) var fra India
 a man that was from India
 'a man that was from India'

Therefore, as Pesetsky points out, the contraction rule, (16) above, is consistent with the fact that relative clause complementizers are morphologically distinct in many languages.

3.1.2. Locality as Antecedent Government

Pesetsky's account crucially assumes that the trace of *wh*-movement is an anaphor, a result which is not compatible with the variable-like properties of *wh*-traces (e.g. strong crossover). Therefore, later work abandons the assumption that the Binding Theory (NIC) can account for the *that*-trace effect. However, the intuition that the complementizer destroys a requisite locality relation between subject traces and their antecedents is preserved under the assumption that traces must be related to their antecedents by a relation of antecedent government and that the complementizer blocks this relation.

One version of this idea is outlined in Chomsky 1986a, who, adopting the definition of proper government in (19) below, further assumes government relations to be subject to the 'Minimality Condition', (20):

(19) *Proper Government*

α properly governs β iff α θ-governs or antecedent-governs β. (Chomsky 1986a: 17)

That is, if δ governs β in the following configuration, then α does not govern β even if it otherwise satisfies the requirements for government (Chomsky 1986a: 10).

(20) *Minimality Condition*

$\alpha ... [_\gamma ... \delta ... \beta ...]$

In the case of long subject movement, the complementizer counts as δ in the above definition, blocking antecedent government of the subject trace from the intermediate trace in the specifier of CP:

(21)a. *Who$_i$ did you believe [$_{CP}$ t_i' [$_{C'}$ that [$_{IP}$ t_i would win]]]?

b. Who$_i$ did you believe [$_{CP}$ t_i' [$_{C'}$ ø [$_{IP}$ t_i would win]]]?

Therefore, the *that*-trace effect reduces to a failure of proper (antecedent) government. Crucially, however, it must be assumed that null complementizers are exceptional and are invisible for minimality purposes. Otherwise, (21)b above would also be predicted to be ungrammatical. However, if it is assumed, as Chomsky proposes, that null complementizers are contentless, featureless elements, then it is plausible that they do not count as an appropriate choice for δ in (20) above. Furthermore, adopting some form of Pesetsky's re-indexing rule, the fact that complementizers in relative clauses do not block the antecedent government relation can be accounted for.

Obviously, the IP-hypothesis leads to a simplification of this locality-based account. In the absence of a CP projection, long subject movement from a clause without that is predicted to be fully grammatical, as nothing interferes with the antecedent government.

3.2. The Head-Government Account

More recent work ascribes the *that*-trace effect not to a failure of locality but to a failure of a head-government requirement (e.g. Aoun *et al.* 1987, Rizzi 1990). As Rizzi's account is the most comprehensive attempt to answer the range of questions surrounding the *that*-trace effect in recent times, it is discussed in detail below.

Rizzi's work details the benefits of adopting a relativized approach to minimality, (22) below, (as opposed to the 'rigid' minimality of Chomsky 1986a, (20) above), the crucial consequence of which (for our purposes) is that heads only act as minimality barriers for head-government, and cannot interfere with the antecedent government of phrasal traces.

(22) *Relativized Minimality*

X α-governs Y only if there is no Z such that
(i) Z is a typical potential α-governor for Y
(ii) Z c-commands Y and does not c-command X.

It follows from this approach to government that antecedent government cannot be relevant to the explanation of the *that*-trace effect, assuming that is a head (C^0):

(23) wh_i ... [$_{CP}$ t_i [$_{C'}$ [$_{C^0}$ that] [$_{IP}$ t_i ...]]]

So what principle is violated by the *that*-trace effect? Rizzi claims that it reflects a violation of the head-government requirement of the conjunctive ECP (Rizzi 1990: 32):

(24) *(Conjunctive) ECP*

A nonpronominal empty category must be
(i) properly head-governed (Formal Licensing)
(ii) antecedent-governed or Theta-governed (Identification).

Assuming that proper head-government is government under strict c-command by an appropriate head, (25), then it follows that the only potential head-governor for subject traces is C^0, as illustrated schematically in (26):[4]

(25) *Proper head-government*

α properly head-governs β if α c-commands β and Relativized Minimality is respected.

(26)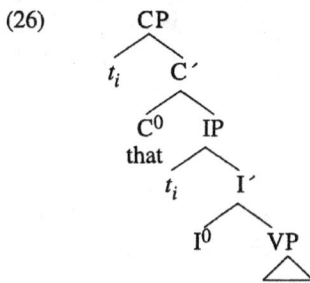

The I^0 head cannot properly head-govern the subject, as it is does not c-command it. Therefore, if C^0 is not a member of the set of proper head governors, subject extraction is excluded. Government from higher heads (such as the matrix verb) is excluded under Relativized Minimality by the intervening C^0. Therefore, the *that*-trace effect reduces to a failure of the proper-head government requirement.

In isolation, this proposal has the effect of excluding subject extraction in all cases, which is too strong a result. Rizzi proposes (1990: 60-65) that UG provides three main strategies to foil this ban on subject extraction. First, the gap position may be filled with a resumptive pronoun, as is the case in Swedish. Secondly, languages such as Italian and Spanish allow the subject to appear in post-verbal position, which is presumably properly head-governed by an inflectional head. Rizzi proposes that the reason for the absence of *that*-trace effects in these languages is that subject extraction proceeds from the properly-governed, post-verbal position.[5] However, neither of these possibilities help to explain why subject extraction in English is possible across null complementizers in the case of long movement and local extraction of subjects:

(27)a. *Who$_i$* do you think [$_{CP}$ t_i [$_{C'}$ ∅ [$_{IP}$ t_i left?]]]

b. *Who$_i$* [$_{C'}$ ∅ [$_{IP}$ t_i left?]]

Within Rizzi's framework of assumptions, outlined above, it must be the case that the null complementizer itself functions as a proper governor for the subject trace in these cases. However, it is not immediately obvious why null complementizers are proper head-governors, while overt complementizers are not. Rizzi's answer is that there is a third mechanism by which subject extraction is licensed: complementizers can themselves become proper head-governors by bearing agreement features, through a process of 'agreement in Comp', discussed in detail below. In English, it is proposed that the morphological realization of these agreement features is generally a null element: [$_{C^0}$ Ø].

3.2.1. Agreement in Comp

As Rizzi points out, many languages display a distinct complementizer form in the case of *wh*-extraction (e.g. French, Irish, Kinande, West Flemish). I illustrate this with French and Irish examples below:

(28) Qui penses-tu (qui/*que) *t* viendra?
 who think-you that will.come
 'Who do you think will come?'

(29) Cé a cheapann tú a (*go) thiocfas?
 who that.wh think you that will-come
 'Who do you think will come?'

Rizzi proposes that this special morphology reflects a specifier-head agreement process between the operator or operator-trace in the specifier of CP and the complementizer. Assuming that UG makes this process available universally, then it is possible that null complementizers in English are simply morphological manifestations of specifier-head agreement. This proposal necessitates relaxing the assumption that Agr always heads its own projection (AgrP) and can be realized as features on a head (Rizzi 1990: 52):

(30) $C^0 \rightarrow$ that
 Agr

Assuming that Agr^0 (and by extension, any head bearing Agr) belongs to the set of proper head-governors, the possibility of subject extraction with null but not overt complementizers follows. Rizzi furthermore proposes that Agr^0 is only a proper governor for elements with which it is co-indexed. In the case of subject extraction, the following elements share an index: the intermediate trace, the subject trace and the complementizer. By specifier-head agreement, the C^0 head shares the index of the subject also. This co-indexing requirement predicts that only agreeing (i.e. null) complementizers may appear in the case of subject extraction.[6] In the case of object extraction, the alternation between *that* and ∅ is also expected, as the object trace does not require head-government from C^0. This explanation is complicated by the apparent reversal of the normal pattern in relative clauses. Subject-gap relatives permit an overt complementizer, while object-gap relatives allow the same alternation between that and ∅ as complement clauses:

(31)a. the key [$_{CP}$ Op_i [$_{C'}$ that [$_{IP}$ t_i opens the chest]]]

   b. the chest [$_{CP}$ Op_i [$_{C'}$ (that / ∅) [$_{IP}$ you opened t_i]]]

Under Rizzi's assumptions it must be the case that the relative complementizer *that* functions as a proper governor in (31)a above. However, this is not particularly worrisome: recall from the discussion of Pesetsky's account above, that many languages use a distinct complementizer for relative clauses.[7]

Therefore, it must be the case that UG offers a formal means of distinguishing the two kinds of complementizer. To this end, Rizzi proposes a feature [+/- predicative]. This feature can be exploited along with the notion of 'agreement in comp' to provide an account for the distribution of complementizers in relatives: the agreeing form of the predicative complementizer is *that*. Therefore, *that* is obligatory with subject-gap relatives but either the agreeing (*that*) or non-agreeing form (∅) can appear with object gaps.[8] The inventory of complementizers for embedded declarative and relative clauses is then as in (32):

(32)a. C^0 +predicative, +Agr = that
   b. C^0 -predicative, +Agr = ∅
   c. C^0 -predicative, -Agr = that
   d. C^0 +predicative, -Agr = ∅

3.2.2. Advantages of the Account

The head-government account is impressive in that it addresses most of the questions related to the *that*-trace effect outlined above. It straightforwardly accounts for the basic data in (1). It is also flexible enough to account for the language-internal variation in the acceptability of *that*-trace violations. As Rizzi points out, an explanation is available if it is assumed that those speakers who allow subject extraction across *that* simply admit *that* as a morphological variant of the agreeing complementizer (Rizzi 1990: 53). As for the question of the cross-linguistic variation in *that*-trace effects, Perlmutter's conjecture is derived, albeit through an independent property of null subject languages: i.e. the possibility of extraction from the post-verbal position. As for the more severe level of ungrammaticality associated with *whether*-trace and *if*-trace effects, these configurations plausibly involve a violation of both clauses of the conjunctive ECP, the antecedent and head-government requirements. Under the assumption that the specifier of CP is filled with an operator in these cases, antecedent government is also blocked by Relativized Minimality. Recall from the previous discussion that the basic *that*-trace effect involves a violation of the head-government requirement only.

3.2.3. Some Difficulties

The basic problem inherent to the head-government account is explaining the possibility of subject extraction across null complementizers. In Rizzi's system, the null complementizer must count as a proper governor. Rizzi's account of this dichotomy is that null complementizers are the morphological realization of an abstract agreement relation. However, it seems that although this proposal is empirically successful, it ultimately rests on a stipulation: there is no explanation here as to why it is the null complementizer which is the proper governor, as opposed to the overt one. The stipulation that null complementizers are proper governors remains: it is simply buried in the morphological component.

Furthermore, there are some difficulties with the mechanism of 'agreement in comp' itself. As pointed out by Frampton (1991: 36-37) two distinct types of agreement appear to be conflated under the rubric of 'agreement in comp.' In languages such as French, the agreement is 'subject-oriented', i.e. there is overt agreement between the C^0 and the subject which is realized as person-number inflection on C^0 (i.e. the *que* → *qui* alternation). However, in languages such as Irish, agreement in Comp is 'specifier-oriented', i.e. there is no evidence of agreement with the extracted subject at all. A special form of C^0 simply appears in the case of *wh*-extraction. As Frampton points out, nothing in Rizzi's system predicts the existence of the latter type of agreement at all.

In the following section, the implications of incorporating the IP-hypothesis into this head-government account are explored. I conclude that the result is a significant reduction in complexity. In particular, appeal to the mechanism of 'agreement in comp' can be abandoned entirely which, given the difficulties outlined above, seems a positive result.

4. IMPLICATIONS FOR THE HEAD-GOVERNMENT ACCOUNT

Under the IP-hypothesis, there are two structural possibilities for long subject movement from finite complement clauses:

(33)a. Who$_i$ do you think [$_{IP}$ t_i left]?

b. *Who$_i$ do you think [$_{CP}$ that [$_{IP}$ t_i left]]?

Therefore, there is no need to appeal to 'agreement in Comp' in these cases to explain the possibility of subject extraction from a *that*-less clause: the subject trace in (33)a is head-governed by the matrix verb: the IP complement is a selected complement and therefore both L-marked and θ-marked. Therefore, it is not a barrier to external government. The ungrammaticality of (33)b is predicted, assuming that C^0 is not a proper governor: the subject trace fails to be properly head-governed, as proper government from the matrix verb is blocked by the intervening complementizer under Relativized Minimality.

The basic cases can be derived under the simple statement in (34):

(34) C^0 [-predicative] is not a proper governor.

Furthermore, recall from Chapter 3 that relative clauses without *that* are analyzed as bare IPs:

(35) The man [$_{IP}$ Mary likes t] is here.

Therefore, as with complement clauses the problem of the government properties of null C^0 in relative clauses does not arise. However, overt C^0 in relative clauses apparently does count as a proper governor:

(36) the man [$_{CP}$ that [$_{IP}$ t likes Mary]]

(37) C^0 [+predicative] is a proper governor.

However, this statement may be unnecessary. Recall from Chapter 3 that IP-relatives may contain subject gaps (albeit under certain restricted circumstances):

(38) There's someone [$_{IP}$ e wants to see you.]

Under Rizzi's assumption that the proper head-governor for the subject trace is C^0, this empty category lacks a proper head-governor. There seem to be two possibilities: either, (i) the head-government requirement holds only of movement-derived variables (traces) not base-generated variables; or (ii) the variable is pronominal and therefore exempt from ECP requirements, following the proposal of Cinque 1990 that A´-chains may terminate in the null pronominal, *pro*.[9]

If either of these general approaches extended to *that*-relatives, the question of how the subject empty category is properly governed would not arise. If such a proposal is tenable, the absence of *that*-trace effects from relative clauses is expected not as a result of the special status of the relative complementizer as a proper governor, but because of the absence of trace. Therefore, it may be possible to maintain the simple statement that overt complementizers are not proper governors in English.[10] However, I propose to leave this question unresolved for now and return to it in 4.2 below.

In sum, the IP-hypothesis permits a significant reduction in the complexity of the head-government account of the *that*-trace effect. In the general absence of zero complementizers, no appeal to morphological accident need be made. Instead, it can be simply maintained that C^0 is not a proper governor (relative clauses aside). However, there is one remaining instance where null complementizers appear to act as proper governors, in the case of local subject *wh*-extraction:

(39)a. [$_{CP}$ Who$_i$ [$_{C'}$ ∅ [$_{IP}$ t_i left?]]]

b. I was wondering [$_{CP}$ who$_i$ [$_{C'}$ ∅ [$_{IP}$ t_i left.]]]

Assuming that the only available head-governor for a subject trace is the complementizer, it seems to be the case that these null complementizers must count as proper governors. Therefore, at first blush, it seems that the question of why null complementizers count as proper governors (and by extension, appeal to a mechanism such as 'agreement in comp') cannot be eliminated entirely from the head-government account.

There are some alternatives, however. First, following a suggestion of Chomsky 1986a, the possibility is explored that null complementizers are compatible with subject traces not because they are proper governors, but simply because they are null, contentless elements which are inert for government theory. Second, the possibility of eliminating the question of the proper government properties of null C^0 entirely, by adopting an *in situ* derivation for local subject extraction is considered.

4.1. Null Complementizers are Inert for Government

Assuming that null complementizers are radically empty nodes devoid of any lexical or inflectional content, it seems natural that they be inert for government purposes:[11]

(40)   *Head Government*

α head-governs β if
α m-commands β, α non-empty.

That is, in the computation of government relations, only lexically-contentful heads are active. Empty heads do not count as an appropriate choice for α in the above definition.

This proposal seems natural. However, it entails that the traces of local subject extraction as in the following examples lack a proper governor entirely, under Rizzi's definitions of proper head-government.

(41)a.   Who$_i$ [$_{CP}$ ∅ [t_i [left]]]?

b.   I wonder [$_{CP}$ who$_i$ [∅ [t_i left]]].

c.   the man [$_{CP}$ who$_i$ [∅ [t_i left]]]

The subject trace in each case is head-governed by I^0 but not c-commanded by it. Therefore, I^0 does not properly govern the trace. The only possible proper governor is the complementizer, which under the above proposal is not a potential head-governor. Therefore, assuming that all traces require proper head-government, these sentences are predicted to be ungrammatical.

If a change in the domain of application of the ECP is adopted, along the lines of Chung 1993, then the desired results may follow, however. Chung 1993 notes that IP-adjoined adverbials in Chamorro systematically escape the head-government requirement of the ECP, while VP-adjoined adverbials do not, and are also required to move in a more local fashion. In order to account for these facts, Chung proposes that not all adjunct traces are subject to the ECP in the same way. In particular, IP-adjoined adverbials are proposed to be exempt from the head-government requirement because they cannot in principle satisfy it, while other traces must satisfy both head and antecedent government (Chung 1993: 16-19):

(42)a. Head government holds at s-structure.
  b. Traces outside the minimal m-command domain of I^0 (i.e. traces adjoined to IP) must satisfy antecedent government. All other traces must satisfy head government and antecedent government.
  c. The ECP is enforced at the earliest point in the derivation at which one of its subparts must be satisfied. If no such point can be identified, then the ECP is enforced at LF.

Putting aside the details of this account, the core idea relevant to the current discussion is the proposal that the head-government requirement of the ECP applies only to a subset of movement traces: those which could, in principle, satisfy it. Although no formalization is offered here, this proposal seems to have some promise in accounting for exceptional behavior of null complementizers: the subject traces in (41) completely lack any potential head-governor, if null C^0 is invisible for government theory. Therefore, it could perhaps be maintained that they are exempt from the head-government requirement because they cannot in principle satisfy it.

This approach involves a quite radical departure from current conceptions of the ECP. However, an alternative explanation is available, for which there is some empirical evidence: if local subject *wh*-extraction involves no syntactic movement at all, the *wh*-word remaining *in situ*, then the question of the proper government properties of null complementizers does not arise.

4.2. Vacuous Movement

Non-movement analyses of local subject *wh*-extraction in which the *wh*-word remains *in situ*, rather than undergoing movement to specifier of CP have been frequently proposed in the literature (e.g. Chomsky 1986a, Chung and McCloskey 1983, George 1980, Grimshaw 1993, Haider 1989). The theoretical motivation for such analyses is diverse. Chomsky (1986a: 48-54) assumes a form of the 'Vacuous Movement Hypothesis' (VMH) of George 1980 stating that string-vacuous movement need not apply in the syntax. This proposal is based on considerations of language acquisition: i.e. the language learner does not posit movement unless there is overt evidence for it. Therefore, an *in situ* syntactic derivation of local subject movement is proposed:

(43)a. [$_{CP}$ Ø [$_{IP}$ What intrigues you?]]

  b. I wonder [$_{CP}$ Ø [$_{IP}$ what intrigues you]].

One pleasing consequence of this approach is that it explains the absence of *do*-support with subject extraction (**Who did leave*).

The location of the *wh*-word in specifier of IP is legitimate assuming that clausal scope for *wh*-operators is demanded only at LF (which is independently suggested by languages which lack overt syntactic *wh*-movement). Furthermore, assuming that selectional properties can be met at LF under government, the selectional requirements of verbs like *wonder* which demand interrogative (+*wh*) complements are not violated, the matrix verb governs the *wh*-phrase in the specifier of its complement (Chomsky 1986a: 52). Furthermore, this analysis has some positive empirical consequences, as discussed by Chomsky (1986a: 50-4), e.g. it provides an account of many of the phenomena discussed in Chung and McCloskey 1983. Consider the following examples:[12]

(44)a. this is a paper [that we need to find [someone [$_{IP}$ who understands t]]]

b. this is a paper [that we need to find [someone [$_{CP}$ Op_j that we can intimidate with t]]]

The contrast in relative acceptability between (44)a and (44)b follows from an *in situ* derivation under the VMH. In (44)a, no filled A′-specifier position intervenes between the trace and its antecedent in the higher clause. However, in (44)b the specifier of CP is filled with the relative operator which binds the trace in the object of *intimidate*. Therefore, the movement of the prepositional complement in this case will induce at least a Subjacency violation.

Under the IP-hypothesis, root and embedded clauses with local subject extraction have the following structures:[13]

(45)a. [$_{IP}$ *Who* [$_{I'}$ left]]?

b. I wonder [$_{IP}$ *who* [$_{I'}$ left]].

As was argued for complement declarative clauses, the alternation between IP and CP in complement position does not pose a problem for the theory of selection. In a theory which admits only s-selection, if both IP and CP are valid realizations of the semantic category 'Proposition' or 'Question', then the alternation between them does not violate the selectional requirements of the verb.[14]

If this general approach is tenable, then the question of the proper government properties of null complementizers can be entirely eliminated. Null complementizers governing subject traces simply do not occur. In fact, the only instance of null complementizers in English occur when a complement or adjunct *wh*-word moves to specifier of CP. Therefore, the head-government account of the *that*-trace effect can be reduced to (at least) the following statement:

(46)a. C^0 [-predicative] is not a proper head-governor.
b. C^0 [+predicative] is a proper governor.

There is some reason to believe, however, that an *in situ* analysis of 'subject-gap' *that*-relatives is possible. Assuming that the element that is ambiguous between being a C^0 head and a relative pronoun, the same considerations which lead to an *in situ* analysis of subject *wh*-relatives dictate an *in situ* derivation:

(47)a. the man [IP *who* [I' opened the door]]

b. the man [IP that [I' opened the door]]

The proposed status of *that* as a relative pronoun is not without precedent: this question has been a long-standing point of contention in traditional grammar.[15] Furthermore, it is noteworthy that the same evidence which supports the VMH analysis of *wh*-relatives carries over to *that*-relatives:

(48)a. this is a paper [that we need to find [someone [IP that understands *t*]]
b. this is a paper [that we need to find [someone [CP Op_j that [IP we can intimidate t_j with *t*]]]

The contrast in relative acceptability between (48)a and (48)b is consistent with the indicated *in situ* derivation: no filled A´-specifier position intervenes between the trace and its landing site in (48)a. However, in (48)b a relative operator occupies the specifier position immediately dominating the trace, ensuring that at least a Subjacency violation occurs.

One immediate concern about the structure in (47)b is that it seems to predict that IP-adjoined adverbs should appear to the left of (pronominal) *that*, which is of course, not the case:

(49) *the man last night that came to dinner

However, recall from Chapter 3 that adjunction of an adverb to the maximal projection of a relative clause modifier is excluded in principle. Therefore, the ungrammaticality of (49) above follows from independent reasons. If this account is tenable, the following maximal reduction of the head-government properties of complementizers obtains:

(50) C^0 is not a proper governor.

This is obviously a significant reduction in the complexity of the previous account.

5. CHAPTER SUMMARY

In conclusion, the IP-hypothesis allows for a considerable reduction in the analytical task posed by the *that*-trace effect. In combination with an *in situ* derivation of local subject extraction (under the VMH) the head-government account can be reduced to the statement in (46) above. Finally, adopting an *in situ* derivation for subject-gap *that*-relatives, the maximally simple statement in (50) is possible.

This streamlined account seems as successful as Rizzi's in accounting for the questions related to the *that*-trace effect outlined in section 2 above. The cross-linguistic and language-internal variation plausibly reflects parametric variation on the status of C^0 as a proper governor. In addition, Rizzi's account of the more severe ungrammaticality associated with *whether*-trace and *if*-trace violations can also be maintained under this approach: if these elements are associated with an operator in specifier of CP, they plausibly involve both a head-government and an antecedent-government violation.

Although this account represents a considerable reduction in the complexity of previous head-government accounts, it is still open to any basic objections which might face government-theoretic accounts, e.g. the 'Adverb Effect' (Culicover 1991, 1993) which seems to indicate that string-adjacency between the complementizer and the subject trace is the determining factor for the *that*-trace effect, not government:

(51)   Robin met the man that Leslie said that for all intents and purposes *t* was mayor of the city.

However, the possibility exists (as pointed out in Culicover 1991) that a 'recursive CP' structure (in the sense of Rizzi and Roberts 1989; Vikner 1991, 1995; McCloskey 1992) may account for the grammaticality of these examples:

(52) V^0 [$_{CP}$ that [$_{CP(=PoIP)}$ *Adverb* [$_{C'}$ ∅ [$_{IP}$ *t* ...]]]

In this structure, the head of the recursive CP (or PolP, in Culicover's terms) is possibly a proper governor for the subject trace. One of the main objections of Culicover 1993 to this structure is that the proposed projection of PolP just in case an adverb fills its specifier is *ad hoc*: if the lower CP in the recursive structure (PolP) were freely generated, then it should always be possible to avoid *that*-trace violations. However, the desired result is actually expected under the IP-hypothesis. As discussed in Chapter 5, the IP-hypothesis entails a minimalist approach to clausal projection: i.e. CP is never vacuously projected. Therefore, the central objection to the recursive CP analysis of the Adverb Effect disappears under the IP-hypothesis. Of course, it is still a question as to why this null head should count as a proper governor.

NOTES

1. Pesetsky (1982a: 328) suggests based on information from Wilson Gray (p.c.) that African American Vernacular English may lack *that*-trace effects entirely.
2. This observation is confirmed, at least for *whether*-trace configurations, by Sobin's 1987 study (Sobin 1987: 46).
3. There are other approaches of course, such as Pesetsky's 1982b Path Containment Condition and Gazdar's 1981 Generalized Left-Branch Condition.
4. Other definitions of proper government are considered. See Rizzi (1990: 31) for discussion.
5. I do not discuss the evidence for this here (cf. Rizzi 1990: 61-65) and references.
6. Frampton (1991: 31-2) argues that the condition that agreeing complementizers must be co-indexed with their governees can easily be dispensed with. The consequences of this condition are to exclude I^0 to C^0 movement with subject extraction and to prevent an agreeing complementizer from saving subject extraction from *wh*-islands:

    (i) *Who did *t* leave?
    (ii) *Who$_j$ do you wonder [$_{CP}$ what$_i$ [$_{C'}$ Ø [t$_j$ did t$_i$?]]

In the first case, movement of I^0 into C^0 is incompatible with the appearance of agreement in C^0. In the second case, the obligatory specifier-head agreement relation prevents proper government of the subject trace t$_j$. However, as Frampton points out, alternative explanations of these effects are available. For example, economy considerations could plausibly exclude (i) above by the same principles which exclude *John did see the movie*. In addition, a condition against crossing A'-dependencies (e.g. the Path

Containment Condition of Pesetsky 1982b) could be invoked to account for (ii). Therefore, it seems that Rizzi's account can survive without the co-indexing condition.
7. Rizzi also points out that many languages use a distinct complementizer for relative clauses: e.g. *wo* in Swiss German, *som* in Scandinavian languages, *?asher* in Modern Hebrew and *?alladhi* in Standard Arabic.
8. Rizzi proposes that the agreement relation which applies in complement clauses cannot be permitted to apply in relative clauses. Otherwise, derivations such as the following (subject contact clauses) will be generally permitted:

(i) *the key *Op* Ø opens the chest

Therefore, he proposes (Rizzi 1990: 69-70) that this problem does not arise if null operators are incapable of determining a specifier-head agreement relation. In relative clauses, therefore, which he assumes to be derived *via* null operator movement, the complementizer comes to bear agreement features not through agreement with the operator in specifier of CP, but through the predication relation which holds between the clause (and by extension, its head C^0) and the modified noun phrase. This move has some support, it is claimed, from the presence of overt agreement relations between the relative head and the complementizer in some languages such as Standard Arabic.
9. Cinque (1990: 98 f.) maintains that a subclass of *wh*-constructions (e.g. parasitic gaps) should be reanalyzed as instantiating a null resumptive pronoun strategy:

the article that we filed *t* without reading *pro*

10. However, this approach is problematic in that other 'complementizer-trace' effects show up in both contact relatives and *that*-relatives:

(i) *the man that you weren't sure whether *t* would stop talking
(ii) *the man you didn't know if *t* would stop talking

Given that *whether*-trace violations are standardly ascribed to the ECP, it would seem that the empty category in these clauses is subject to this principle.
11. The exact proposal of Chomsky (1986a: 47-8) is that null complementizers are inert for minimality and not government relations.
12. Chomsky's (112)a,b.
13. This structure is also proposed in Grimshaw (1993: 32-34).

14. Under the Type-Category theory of selection proposed in Grimshaw 1991, an IP with a +*wh* specifier is selectionally equivalent to a CP with a +*wh* specifier. Therefore, the appearance of V^0 with an IP complement in (45)b is unproblematic.
15. See Van der Auwera 1985 for a summary of the arguments. Perlmutter 1971 also proposes that in subject-gap relatives *that* functions as a subject.

CHAPTER 5

Concluding Remarks

1. INTRODUCTION

This work has argued for the IP-hypothesis of the structure of finite argument and relative clauses lacking complementizers. This argument was based on both conceptual and empirical grounds: on conceptual grounds in that the required alternation between null and overt heads in complement clauses is anomalous in broader perspective and on empirical grounds in that the CP-hypothesis makes incorrect predictions about adjunction possibilities while in each case the IP-hypothesis provides a ready account.

The IP-hypothesis has some broad theoretical consequences. In particular, it lends strong support to the position taken by Chomsky 1986a and Gazdar *et al.* 1985 that 'S' is a maximal projection. However, the IP-hypothesis also has more specific theoretical and empirical consequences which were investigated in the three major chapters of this book.

The analysis of *that*-less argument clauses as bare finite IP is incompatible with the classical ECP analysis of their distribution in terms of a proper government requirement on null complementizers (Stowell 1981). However, it was shown in Chapter 2 that this classical analysis is problematic from both a conceptual and empirical viewpoint; conceptually because it is not clear why null complementizers require proper government; empirically because the analysis predicts that the set of clauses whose complementizer heads are properly governed should be identical to the set of clauses which allow *that* to be absent. It was demonstrated that although these sets overlap in the general case, there are instances of null complementizers which cannot be properly governed, under standard conceptions (e.g. in *wh*-relatives and degree clauses) and instances of properly governed complementizers which cannot be null (in embedded sentential subjects). Therefore, it was concluded that the loss of this account is not as serious an objection to the IP-hypothesis as might seem at first.

In Chapter 3, it was shown that the proposed analysis of *that*-less relatives (contact clauses) as finite IP modifiers is compatible with current assumptions about the structure and interpretation of relative clauses: the proposed representational A´-chain between the relative head and the gap accounts for the basic similarities between contact clauses and other relative clauses. Furthermore, this binding relation provides the basis of a plausible structural account of the adjacency constraints on these relative clauses.

Thirdly, the proposal of IP-complementation has consequences for extraction theory, in particular, the problem of accounting for the *that*-trace effect can be considerably diminished. As outlined in Chapter 4, in combination with an *in situ* derivation for local subject extraction (Chomsky 1986a) the head-government account can be maximally reduced to the simple statement that C^0 is not a proper governor in English, which is a pleasing reduction of the complexity of previous accounts.

2. DISTRIBUTION OF NON-ROOT IP

The question which is perhaps least resolved under the IP-hypothesis is the proper account of the distribution of *that*-less clauses (now analyzed as bare IP). It was suggested, based on the observation that IP always appears as a complement to X^0 (=C^0, V^0...), that the principles which determine the syntactic realization of selected semantic categories demand that the canonical structural realization of 'Proposition' (denoted by IP) demand that IP be a complement to a head. This proposal has the advantage of permitting the distributional constraints on argument IP to be captured while still admitting IP as an adjunct (as a relative clause or degree clause), under the assumption that non-arguments are not subject to canonical structural realization requirements. The question which remains, however, is exactly why selected IP is subject to this restriction to complement positions.

This is one approach to the data. There are certainly others. A notable property of the present account is that the distributional requirements on argument IP and on IP-relatives follow from entirely different sets of considerations. In the latter case, it is the required integrity of the A´-binding relation between the relative head and the gap which is responsible for the adjacency restrictions on this construction. An alternative approach, however, is that the distributional constraints on argument IP and IP-relatives both follow from the same source, perhaps from some inherent property of IP. One possibility is that IP belongs to a set of categories which are syntactically dependent in that they always appear as the complement of (some) head.[1] In particular, NP and VP are plausibly of this type: the assumption that noun phrases (in argument positions at least) are always DP entails that NP never appears outside the complement of D^0. Furthermore, it is also the case that VP always appears as a complement to I^0 (or one of its subcomponents). Therefore, it is possibly the case that IP is not alone in its restriction to head-complement position: other syntactic categories, namely NP and VP are similarly restricted. An explanation of this restriction may lie in the theory of extended projections (Grimshaw 1991). In Grimshaw's system, NP and DP form the extended nominal projection: i.e. they share categorial features and differ only in functional features. DP is the maximal level of this extended projection. Likewise, VP, IP and CP form the extended verbal projection. CP is the maximal level. Therefore, if it is tenable that only maximal extended projections (e.g. CP and DP) can function as arguments outside the head-complement relation, or undergo syntactic movement, then the major distributional characteristics of non-root IP may be accounted for, or at least reduced to the independently necessary question of why NP and VP are subject to similar constraints.

While this line of analysis seems promising for the distributional restrictions on argument IP, it seems to face an insuperable problem in that degree clauses and relative clauses (under standard assumptions) are not head-complements. That is, the restriction of argument IP to head-complement positions cannot reflect something as 'deep' as phrase-structural concerns. Otherwise, the appearance of IP as a degree clause or relative clause should also be excluded by the same considerations.

3. EXTENSION TO BARE INFINITIVES

If the IP-hypothesis is maintained, then it must also be maintained that structures such as the following are excluded:

(1)　　*CP
　　　／＼
　　　ø　C´
　　　　／＼
　　　 C^0　IP
　　　 ø

If CP were permitted to project vacuously, containing no overt material, then alternative analyses of the constructions considered in this work would always exist, and the evidence in favor of the IP-hypothesis would not be accounted for.

It is an interesting question therefore, as to how the projection of empty CP can be ruled out. The most obvious answer, and one which has a strong affinity with the recent move towards a minimalist approach to syntax, is that this projection violates principles of economy. In a system which permits IP-complementation, the null structure in (1) serves no obvious interpretive function and therefore, is plausibly excluded by economy considerations.[2]

The IP-hypothesis, therefore commits to the non-projection of CP in the absence of overt evidence, as in the case of *wh*-movement to specifier of CP. While, this work is exclusively concerned with the IP-hypothesis for finite clauses, clearly the same considerations which lead to the exclusion of (1) above for finite clauses should also extend to the nonfinite domain: i.e. the IP-hypothesis should extend to bare infinitives.[3]

An immediate consequence of the extension of the IP-hypothesis to bare infinitives is that it is incompatible with the Chomsky 1981 (LGB) analysis of the distribution of PRO in terms of government, as in the absence of a null CP projection, the structural requirements for government from the matrix verb are satisfied:

(2) He tried [$_{IP}$ PRO to say that.]

We are committed, therefore, to alternative accounts of the distribution of PRO. One possibility is that of Bouchard 1984 who proposes that the relevant consideration is Case-assignment: i.e. PRO is excluded from Case-marked positions. Therefore, the loss of the LGB account may not pose an insurmountable problem.

This extension also has obvious consequences for the LGB account of the relative distribution of ECM and PRO. Following Bresnan 1972, it is proposed that certain verbs take IP-complements while others take CP-complements. In general, the proposed distinction is that verbs which take CP complements admit PRO, but not ECM (e.g. *try*), (3). Verbs which take IP-complements (derived through a process of 'S´-deletion') allow ECM but not PRO, (4).

(3)a. *I tried [$_{CP}$ him to leave.]
   b. I tried [$_{CP}$ PRO to leave.]

(4)a. I believe [$_{IP}$ him to be silly.]
   b. *I believe [$_{IP}$ PRO to be interesting.]

However, the verb *want* is anomalous under this approach in that it permits both ECM and PRO.[4] Therefore, it is proposed that this verb takes a CP-complement which contains a deleted Case-marking *for*-complementizer, giving the form of an ECM construction:

(5)a. I want [CP ∅ [IP him to leave.]

b. I want [CP PRO to leave.]

However, if all bare infinitive complements are IP, then obviously, the relative distribution of ECM and PRO cannot be maintained in terms of IP-complementation *versus* CP-complementation. While many unresolved questions remain, it is possible that the IP-hypothesis solves the problem posed by *want*: if the relative distribution of ECM and PRO is not determined by considerations of complementation, then it is perhaps less surprising that they are not in complementary distribution.

Furthermore, it is interesting that there are many distributional parallels between finite IPs and bare infinitives. In particular, bare infinitives appear in all the syntactic positions in which finite IP appears and are also excluded from many of the environments from which finite IP is excluded. In particular, just like finite IP, bare infinitives (obviously) appear as verb-complements, as is discussed above. However, they also appear as degree clauses and as relative clauses, as in (6) and (7), respectively:

(6)a. It's too wet [to go running on the trails.]
b. John is clever enough [to solve this problem.]

(7) The man [to fix the sink] is here.

Furthermore, bare infinitives are excluded from many of the environments from which finite IPs are excluded. For example, manner of speech verbs seem to reject bare infinitive complements, while they admit nonfinite CP complements:

(8)a. I said [for someone to turn off the stereo.]
b. I yelled [for someone to turn off the stereo.]

c. I said [to turn off the stereo.]
d. *I yelled [to turn off the stereo.]

Furthermore, like finite IP-relatives (contact clauses) infinitival relatives cannot 'stack' or extrapose:[5]

(9)a. A philanthropist to talk to who is wealthy called this afternoon.
   b. *A philanthropist who is wealthy to talk to called this afternoon.

(10)a. One wealthy philanthropist called today who you should talk to.
    b. *One wealthy philanthropist called today to talk to.

Therefore, there are some parallels in the distribution of finite IP and bare infinitives. There are also some interesting differences. In particular, bare infinitives appear in some non-complement positions from which finite IP is excluded, e.g. subject position, (11). They also appear as non-selected purpose clauses, (12):

(11)a. [To eat meat on a fast day] is sinful.
    b. [To walk home in the rain] is depressing.
    c. [To meet new people] is nice.

(12)a. He bought it [to drive to work in.]
    b. He married her [to get a green card.]
    c. I gave a book to Mary [to make her happy.]

In sum, the adoption of the IP-hypothesis in the finite domain seems to necessitate a similar approach to the syntax of bare infinitive clauses. Although the full implications of this proposal cannot be explored in any detail here, we have determined that there are some initial indications that the extension of the IP-hypothesis to the nonfinite domain may be fruitful.

NOTES

1. See Svenonius 1994, Chapter 3 for a development of the notion of dependent categories.
2. These considerations tell against another possible approach to the evidence in favor of IP-complementation: i.e. that there is a process of *that*-deletion (or base generation of null complementizers) which is accompanied by obligatory pruning of the remaining null CP-structure.
3. See Bošković 1996 and 1997 for an extension of the IP-hypothesis to non-finite clauses.
4. Other verbs of this class are *desire, need, wish*, reported by Pesetsky (1991: 21).
5. These examples are taken from Kirkpatrick 1982. Thanks to Sandy Chung for drawing my attention to these facts.

Bibliography

Abney, Steven. 1987. *The English Noun Phrase in its Sentential Aspect*. Ph.D. dissertation, MIT.
Aoun, Joseph. 1985. *A Grammar of Anaphora*. Cambridge, Massachusetts: MIT Press.
Aoun, Joseph, Hornstein, Norbert, Lightfoot, David and Amy Weinberg. 1987. Two Types of Locality. *Linguistic Inquiry* 18: 537-577.
Authier, Jean-Marc. 1992. Iterated CPs and embedded topicalization. *Linguistic Inquiry* 23: 329-336.
Auwera, Johan van der. 1984. More on the History of Subject Contact Clauses in English. *Folia Linguistica Historica* 5: 171-184.
—————— 1985. Relative *that*: a centennial dispute. *Journal of Linguistics* 21: 149-179.
Baker, Mark 1988. *Incorporation: a theory of grammatical function changing*. Chicago: University of Chicago Press.
Barwise, Jon and Robin Cooper. 1981. Generalized Quantifiers and Natural Language. *Linguistics & Philosophy* 4: 159-219.
Bever, Thomas G. and D. Terence Langendoen. 1971. A Dynamic Model of the Evolution of Language. *Linguistic Inquiry* 2: 433-463.
Bianchi, Valentina 1991. Le relative infinitive e altre strutture modali infinitive in Italiano. *Quaderni del Laboratorio di Linguistica* 5: 105-127. Pisa: Scuola Normale Superiore.
Bolinger, Dwight 1972. *That's That*. Janua Linguarum Series Minor, 155. The Hague: Mouton.
Bošković, Željko. 1994. Categorial Status of Null Operator Relatives and Finite Declarative Complements. *Language Research* 30: 387-417.
—————— 1996. Selection and the Categorial Status of Nonfinite Complements. *Natural Language and Linguistic Theory* 14: 269-304.
—————— 1997. *The Syntax of Nonfinite Complementation: An Economy Approach*. Linguistic Inquiry Monograph 32. Cambridge, Massachusetts: MIT Press.
Bouchard, Denis 1984. *On the Content of Empty Categories*. Dordrecht: Foris.
Bowers, John. 1987. Extended X-bar Theory, the ECP and the Left Branch Condition. In *Proceedings of the Sixth West Coast Conference on Formal Linguistics*, edited by Megan Crowhurst, 47-62. Stanford, CA: CSLI Publications [Distributed by Cambridge University Press].

Bowers, John S. 1968. Adjectives and Adverbs in English. Indiana University Linguistics Club. [1975] *Foundations of Language* 13: 529-562.

Bresnan, Joan. 1970. On Complementizers: Toward a Syntactic Theory of Complement Types. *Foundations of Language* 6: 297-321.

——— 1972. *Theory of Complementation in English Syntax*. Ph.D. dissertation, MIT. [1979]. Outstanding Dissertations in Linguistics. New York: Garland.

——— 1982. Control and Complementation. *Linguistic Inquiry* 13: 343-434.

Carlson, Gregory N. 1981. The Distribution of Free-Choice Any. In *Papers from the Seventeenth Meeting of the Chicago Linguistic Society*, edited by Roberta A. Hendrick *et al.* Chicago: Chicago Linguistic Society.

Chomsky, Noam 1970. Remarks on Nominalization. In *Readings on English Transformational Grammar*, edited by Roderick A. Jacobs and Peter S. Rosenbaum, 184-221. Waltham, Massachusetts: Ginn and Co.

——— 1977. On WH-Movement. In *Formal Syntax*, edited by Peter W. Culicover, Thomas Wasow and Adrian Akmajian, 71-132. San Diego: Academic Press.

——— 1981. *Lectures on Government and Binding*. Studies in Generative Grammar 9. Dordrecht: Foris.

——— 1986a. *Barriers*. Linguistic Inquiry Monograph Thirteen. Cambridge, Massachusetts: MIT Press.

——— 1986b. *Knowledge of Language: Its Nature Origin and Use*. New York: Praeger.

——— 1992. *A Minimalist Program for Linguistic Theory*. MIT Working Papers in Linguistics.

——— 1995. *The Minimalist Program*. Cambridge, Massachusetts: MIT Press.

Chomsky, Noam and Howard Lasnik 1977. Filters and Control. *Linguistic Inquiry* 8: 425-504.

——— and ——— 1993. Principles and Parameters Theory. In *Syntax: an International Handbook of Contemporary Research*, edited by Joachim Jacobs *et al.*, 506-569. Berlin: de Gruyter.

Chung, Sandra 1990. VP's and Verb Movement in Chamorro. *Natural Language and Linguistic Theory* 8: 559-619.

——— 1993. Extraction of Nonarguments in Chamorro. Linguistics Research Center. University of California, Santa Cruz.

Chung, Sandra and James McCloskey. 1983. On the Interpretation of Certain Island Effects in GPSG. *Linguistic Inquiry* 14: 704-713.

Cinque, Guglielmo. 1990. *Types of A-Bar Dependencies*. Linguistic Inquiry Monograph 17. Cambridge, Massachusetts: MIT Press.

Culicover, Peter W. 1991. Topicalization, inversion and complementizers in English. In *Going Romance and Beyond*, edited by Denis Delfitto, Martin Everaert, Arnold Evers and Frits Stuurman, 1-43. University of Utrecht: OTS Working Papers.

────── 1993. Evidence against ECP accounts of the *that*-t effect. *Linguistic Inquiry* 24: 557-561.

Curme, George. O. 1931. *Syntax*. D.C. and New York: Heath and Company.

Doherty, Cathal. 1993. The Syntax of Subject Contact Relatives. Paper presented at the Twenty-Ninth Meeting of the Chicago Linguistic Society, April 1993. [1994] In *Proceedings of the Twenty-Ninth Annual Meeting of the Chicago Linguistic Society*, edited by Katharine Beals *et al.*, 55-65. Chicago: Chicago Linguistic Society.

────── 1997. Clauses without complementizers: Finite IP-complementation in English. *The Linguistic Review* 14: 197-220.

Dubinksy, Stanley and Kemp Williams. 1995. Recategorization as Complementizers: The Case of Temporal Prepositions in English. *Linguistic Inquiry* 26: 125-137.

Engdahl, Elisabet. 1981. Parasitic Gaps. *Linguistics and Philosophy* 6: 211-243.

Erdmann, Peter. 1980. On the History of Subject Contact-Clauses in English. *Folia Linguistica Historica* 1: 139-170.

Erteschik, Nomi. 1973. *On the Nature of Island Constraints*. Ph.D. dissertation. MIT. [1977] Indiana University Linguistics Club.

Fiengo, Robert. 1977. On Trace Theory. *Linguistic Inquiry* 8: 35-81.

Frampton, John. 1991. Relativized Minimality, A Review. *The Linguistic Review* 8: 1-46.

Gazdar, Gerald. 1981. Unbounded dependencies and coordinate structures. *Linguistic Inquiry* 12: 115-84.

Gazdar, Gerald, Klein, Ewan, Pullum, Geoffrey K. and Ivan Sag. 1985. *Generalized Phrase Structure Grammar*. Oxford: Basil Blackwell.

George, Leland. 1980. *Analogical Generalization in Natural Language Syntax*. Ph.D. dissertation. MIT.

Goodluck, Helen. 1997. Relative clauses in the speech of Adam. In *Proceedings of the GALA '97 Conference on Language Acquisition*, edited by Antonella Sorace, Caroline Heycock, and Richard Shillcock, 51-56. Edinburgh, UK: Human Communications Research Centre, University of Edinburgh.

Grimshaw, Jane. 1979. Complement Selection and the Lexicon. *Linguistic Inquiry* 10: 279-326.

────── 1981. Form, Function and the Language Acquisition Device. In *The Logical Problem of Language Acquisition*, edited by C.L. Baker and John J. McCarthy, 165-182. Cambridge, Massachusetts: MIT Press.

────── 1990. *Argument Structure*. Linguistic Inquiry Monograph Eighteen. Cambridge, Massachusetts: MIT Press.

────── 1991. Extended Projections. ms. Brandeis University.

────── 1993. Minimal Projection, Heads, and Optimality. ms. Rutgers University: Rutgers Optimality Archive.

────── 1997. Projection, Heads and Optimality. *Linguistic Inquiry* 28: 373-422.

Haider, Hubert. 1987. Matching Projections. In *Constituent Structure: Papers from the 1987 GLOW conference*, edited by Anna Cardinaletti, Guglielmo Cinque and Giuliana Giusti, 101-123. Dordrecht: Foris.

Hankamer, Jorge. 1979. *Deletion in Coordinate Structures*. Outstanding Dissertations in Linguistics. New York: Garland.
Harris, Martin and Nigel Vincent. 1980. On Zero Relatives. *Linguistic Inquiry* 11: 805-807.
Hegarty, Michael. 1991. *Adjunct Extraction and Chain Configurations*. MIT Ph.D. dissertation.
Henry, Alison. 1995. *Belfast English and Standard English: Dialect Variation and Parameter Setting*. Oxford Studies in Comparative Syntax. Oxford University Press.
Hornstein, Norbert and David Lightfoot. 1992. On the Nature of Lexical Government. In *Principles and Parameters in Comparative Grammar*, edited by Robert Freiden, 365-391. Cambridge, Massachusetts: MIT Press.
Huang, James. 1982. *Logical Relations in Chinese and the Theory of Grammar*. Ph.D. dissertation, MIT.
Jackendoff, Ray. 1977. *X-bar Syntax*: A Study of Phrase Structure. MIT Press.
Jespersen, Otto. 1909-49. *A Grammar of English on Historical Principles*, Volume III. London: George Allen & Unwin Ltd.
Kayne, Richard. 1981a. ECP Extensions. *Linguistic Inquiry* 12: 93-133.
——— 1981b. On Certain Differences between French and English. *Linguistic Inquiry* 12: 349-371.
——— 1984. *Connectedness and Binary Branching*. Dordrecht: Foris.
Keenan, Edward. 1987. A Semantic Definition of 'Indefinite NP'. In *The Representation of (In)definiteness*, edited by Eric J. Reuland and Alice G.B. ter Meulen, 286-317. Cambridge, Massachusetts: MIT Press.
Kirkpatrick, Charles. 1982. A Note on Purpose Clauses. In *Proceedings of the First West Coast Conference on Formal Linguistics*, edited by Daniel Flickinger *et al.*, 268-279. Stanford.
Koopman, Hilda and Dominique Sportiche. 1982. Variables and the Bijection Principle. *The Linguistic Review* 2: 139-160.
Ladusaw, William. 1979. *Negative Polarity as Inherent Scope Relations*. Ph.D. dissertation, University of Texas at Austin. [1980] Outstanding Dissertations in Linguistics. New York: Garland.
Lasnik, Howard and Mamoru Saito. 1992. *Move-alpha: Conditions on Its Application and Output*. Current Studies in Linguistics. MIT Press.
Legendre, Géraldine, Smolensky, Paul and Colin Wilson. 1998. When is Less More?. In *Is the Best Good Enough?: Optimality and Competition in Syntax*, edited by Pilar Barbosa *et al.*, 249-289. Cambridge, Massachusetts: MIT Press.
Lodge, Ken R. 1979. A Three-Dimensional Analysis of Non-Standard English. *Journal of Pragmatics* 3: 169-195.
Longobardi, Giuseppe. 1991. Proper Names and the Theory of N-movement in *Syntax and Logical Form*. University of Venice Working Papers in Linguistics. [1994] Reference and Proper Names: a theory of N-movement in syntax and Logical Form, *Linguistic Inquiry* 25: 609-65.
Maling, Joan and Annie Zaenen. 1978. The Nonuniversality of a Surface Filter. *Linguistic Inquiry* 9: 475-497.

McCawley, James. 1981. The Syntax and Semantics of English Relative Clauses. *Lingua* 53: 99-149.
────── 1988. *The Syntactic Phenomena of English*. 2 vols. Chicago: University of Chicago Press.
McCloskey, James. 1990. Resumptive Pronouns, A′-Binding and Levels of Representation in Irish. In *The Syntax of the Modern Celtic Languages*. Syntax and Semantics 23, edited by Randall Hendrick, 199-248. San Diego: Academic Press.
────── 1991. Clause Structure, ellipsis and proper government in Irish. *Lingua* 85: 259-302.
────── 1992. Adjunction, Selection and Embedded Verb Second. Linguistics Research Center. University of California, Santa Cruz.
McDavid, Virginia. 1964. The Alternation of 'That' and Zero in Noun Clauses. *American Speech* 39: 102-113.
McNally, Louise. 1992. *An Interpretation for the English Existential Construction*, Ph.D. dissertation, University of California, Santa Cruz. [1997] *A Semantics for the English existential construction*. Outstanding Dissertations in Linguistics. New York: Garland.
Melvold, Janis L. 1991. Factivity and Definiteness. *More Papers on WH-Movement*. MIT Working Papers in Linguistics Vol. 15, edited by Lisa Cheng and Hamida Demirdash, 97-117.
Müller, Gereon and Wolfgang Sternefeld. 1994. Improper movement and Unambiguous Binding. *Linguistic Inquiry* 24: 461-507.
Nagucka, Ruta. 1980. Grammatical Peculiarities of the Contact Clause in Early Modern English. *Folia Historica Linguistica* 1: 171-184.
Perlmutter, David. 1971. *Deep and Surface Structure Constraints in Syntax* New York: Holt, Rinehart and Winston.
Pesetsky, David. 1982a. Complementizer-Trace Phenomena and the Nominative Island Condition. *The Linguistic Review* 1: 297-343.
────── 1982b. *Paths and Categories*. Ph.D. dissertation. MIT.
────── 1991. *Infinitives*. ms. MIT
Prince, Ellen F. 1981. Toward a Taxonomy of Given-New Information. In *Radical Pragmatics*, edited by Peter Cole, 223-55. San Diego: Academic Press.
Pullum, Geoffrey K. 1985. Assuming Some Version of the X-Bar Theory. In *Proceedings of the Twenty-First Annaual Meeting of the Chicago Linguistic Society,* edited by William H. Eilfort *et al.*, 323-353 Chicago: Chicago Linguistic Society.
Quirk, Randolph, Sidney Greenbaum, Geoffrey Leech and Jan Svartvik. 1972. *A Grammar of Contemporary Spoken English*. New York: Harcourt Brace Jovanovich, Inc.
Radford, Andrew. 1997. *Syntactic Theory and the structure of English: A minimalist approach*. Cambridge Textbooks in Linguistics. Cambridge University Press.
Reinhart, Tanya. 1980. On the Position of Extraposed Clauses. *Linguistic Inquiry* 11: 621-624.
Rizzi, Luigi. 1990. *Relativized Minimality*. Linguistic Inquiry Monograph 16. MIT Press.

―――― 1992. Residual Verb Second and the Wh-Criterion. ms. Université de Genève. [1996] In *Parameters and Functional Heads: Essays in Comparative Syntax*, edited by Adriana Belletti and Luigi Rizzi, 63-90. Oxford Studies in Comparative Syntax. Oxford University Press.

Rizzi, Luigi and Ian Roberts. 1989. Complex Inversion in French. *Probus* 1: 1-30.

Rochemont, Michael. 1989. Topic Islands and the Subjacency Parameter. *Canadian Journal of Linguistics/Revue canadienne de Linguistique* 34: 145-170.

Ross, John Robert. 1967. *Constraints on Variables in Syntax*. Ph.D. dissertation, MIT.

Rothstein, Susan D. 1991. Syntactic Licensing and Subcategorization. In *Perspectives on Phrase Structure: Heads and Licensing*. Syntax and Semantics 25, edited by Susan D. Rothstein, 139-157. San Diego: Academic Press.

Safir, Kenneth. 1982. *Syntactic Chains and the Definiteness Effect*. Ph.D. dissertation, MIT.

―――― 1986. Relative Clauses in a Theory of Binding and Levels. *Linguistic Inquiry* 17: 663-689.

Saito, Mamoru. 1992. Long Distance Scrambling in Japanese. *Journal of East Asian Linguistics* 1: 69-118.

Smith, Carlota. 1964. Determiners and Relative Clauses in a Generative Grammar of English. *Language* 40: 37-52.

Sobin, Nicholas. 1987. The Variable Status of Comp-trace Phenomena. *Natural Language and Linguistic Theory* 5: 33-60.

Stockwell, Robert, Schachter, Paul and Barbara Hall Partee. 1973. *The Major Syntactic Structures of English*. New York: Holt, Rinehart and Winston, Inc.

Stowell, Timothy A. 1978. What was There Before There was There. In *Proceedings of the Fourteenth Annual Meeting of the Chicago Linguistic Society*, edited by Donka Farkas *et al.*, 458-471. Chicago: Chicago Linguistic Society.

―――― 1980. Subjects Across Categories. ms. MIT [1983] *The Linguistic Review* 2: 285-312.

―――― 1981. *Origins of Phrase Structure*. Ph.D. dissertation. MIT.

Taraldsen, Knut Tarald. 1980. On the Nominative Island Condition, Vacuous Application and the *That*-trace Filter. Indiana University Linguistics Club.

Vikner, Sten. 1991. *Verb Movement and the Licensing of NP-Positions in the Germanic Languages*. Ph.D. dissertation. University of Stuttgart.

―――― 1995. *Verb Movement and Expletive Subjects in the Germanic Languages*. Oxford Studies in Comparative Syntax. Oxford University Press.

Visser, Fredericus Theodorus. 1963. *An historical syntax of the English language. Part One: syntactical units with one verb*. Leiden: E. J. Brill.

Webelhuth, Gert. 1992. *Principles and Parameters of Syntactic Saturation*. Oxford Studies in Comparative Syntax. Oxford University Press.

Weisler, Steven. 1980. The Syntax of *That*-Less Relatives. *Linguistic Inquiry* 11: 624-631.
Williams, Edwin. 1978. Across-the-board rule application. *Linguistic Inquiry* 9: 31-43.
———— 1984. *There*-Insertion. *Linguistic Inquiry* 15: 131-153.
———— 1987. NP Trace in Theta Theory. *Linguistics and Philosophy* 10: 433-47.
Wolfram, Walt and Donna Christian. 1976. *Appalachian Speech*. Arlington, Virginia: Center for Applied Linguistics.

Index

A'-chain, in contact clauses, 9, 64-67; diagnostics for, 64; without movement, 66-67; and null operator, 65-66
Abney, Steven, 32, 51n.8, 53n.27, 96n.9
Across the Board movement (ATB), and C^0 incorporation, 21-24.
Adjunction Prohibition, 14, 50n.2, 99n.33
Adverb Effect, 121-2
African American Vernacular English (AAVE). *See* English
Agreement in Comp, 104, 112-114
Aoun, Joseph, 18, 24, 26, 30, 69, 104, 110
AP, as subject, 37
Arabic, Standard 123n.7-8
Asyndetic relative clause. *See* Subject contact clause
Authier, Jean-Marc, 13
Auwera, Johan van der, 71, 105, 124n.15
Baker, Mark, 51n.9
Bare plurals, 51n.8
Barwise, Jon, 75
Bavarian, 105
Bever, Thomas G. 98n.24, 102n.47
Bianchi, Valentina, 97n.14
Bijection Principle, 69
Bolinger, Dwight, 47, 54n.36, 55n.42, 73
Bošković, Željko, 10n.3, 52n.13, 97n.13, 130n.3
Bouchard, Denis, 128

Bowers, John, 10n.3
Bowers, John S., 53n.24
Bresnan, Joan, 3-5, 28, 106, 128
Carlson, Gregory, 100n.41
Category (C-)selection, 7, 41
Chamorro, 117
Chomsky, Noam, 3, 5, 6, 7, 10, 11, 13, 18, 28, 50n.2, 53n.21, 57, 67, 73, 96n.2, 97n.17, 98n.21, 103-4, 106, 107, 109, 118-9, 123n.11-2, 125-6, 128
Christian, Donna, 96n.1
Chung, Sandy, 4, 98n.27, 99n.33, 117-9, 130n.5
Cinque, Guglielmo, 43, 46, 97n.15, 98n.26, 101n.43, 116, 123n.9
Comp Contraction, 108. *See also* Que/qui alternation
Contact Clauses, 8, 34, 57-102; A'-chain in, 64-67; absence of pied-piping in, 65-6; adjacency requirement, 59-60; adjunction evidence for IP analysis of, 62-63; *de dicto* and *de re* readings, 91-92; empty category as *pro*, 86, 97n.15; explaining the adjacency requirement, 67-70. *See also* Subject contact clause
Cooper, Robin, 75
Co-ordination, of contact clauses and other relatives, 60; of distinct syntactic categories, 40-41; of subject contact clauses and other relatives, 86-87; of *that* and *that*-less complements, 23

Co-ordinate Structure Constraint (CSC), and C^0 incorporation, 21
CP, vacuous projection of, 127-8
CP-hypothesis, conceptual issues, 5-7; empirical evidence against for *that*-less complements, 12-18; relative clauses, 62-70
Culicover, Peter W., 13, 97n.11, 121-2
Curme, George, 98n.21
Degree clauses, 32-33, 53n.27
Doherty, Cathal, 91, 97n.15, 101n.43
Doubly-Filled Comp Filter, 52n.10, 96n.2, 107
Dubinsky, Stanley, 29
Dutch, 105
Empty Category Principle (ECP), 8; and Chamorro, 117-8; conjunctive 18, 85, 110; and distribution of null C^0, 19-33
Embedded Sentential Subjects, 27-9
Engdahl, Elisabet, 64
English, African American Vernacular (AAVE), 73, 122n.1; Appalachian, 87, 100n.40; British, 71; Hiberno-English, 71, 87, 98n.22, 100n.40; North American, 71, 105
Erdmann, Peter, 58, 71, 73, 89, 90
Erteschick, Nomi, 42, 55n.41, n.45
Exceptional Case Marking (ECM) verbs, 28; 128-9; incorporation analysis, 51n.9
Existential sentences, non-constituency of postcopular DP and coda, 75-77; small clause analysis of, 79-80; subject contact clauses in, 77-82
Extended projection, 8, 127
External Argument Universal (EAU), 34, 37-38
Extent clauses. *See* Degree clauses
Extraposition from NP, 59; of subject contact clauses, 82-83
Factive verbs, 55n.45

Fiengo, Robert, 97n.17
Fixed Subject Constraint, 106
Frampton, John, 114, 122n.6
French, 104, 108, 112, 114
Gapping, 10n.2, 24
Gazdar, Gerald, 7, 54n.34, 122n.3, 125
Generalized Left Branch Condition, 122n.3
George, Leland, 10, 118
Goodluck, Helen, 97n.15
Government Transparency Corollary (GTC), 51-2n.9
Gray, Wilson, 98n.23, 122n.1
Grimshaw, Jane, 7, 10n.3, 39-40, 44, 49, 53n.21,n.30, 65, 104, 118, 123n.13, 124n.14, 127
Guasti, Giuliana, 98n.21
Haider, Hubert, 118
Hankamer, Jorge, 10n.2
Harris, Martin, 85, 100n.37
Head Government, 19; at Phonological Form, 24-27; Proper, 18, 111. *See also* Empty Category Principle
Hebrew, Modern, 123n.7
Hegarty, Michael, 55n.45
Henry, Alison, 89, 100-1n.42
Hiberno-English. *See* English
Highest Subject Constraint. *See* Resumptive pronouns
Hornstein, Norbert, 24-27, 30-31
Huang, James, 29
Icelandic, 105
Internal NP over S Constraint, 36, 52n.16
IP, as category of S(entence), 3-4; syntactic distribution, 33-40; 126-7
IP-hypothesis, conceptual issues, 5-9; and Control, 128; and ECP, 18-33; empirical evidence for *that*-less complements, 12-8; evidence for contact clauses, 62-70; extension to bare infinitives, 10, 127-130
Irish, 105, 112, 114

Index

Italian, 51n.8, 97n.14, 105, 111
Jackendoff, Ray, 3, 4, 32, 53n.24, 55n.40, 84
Jespersen, Otto, 8, 57, 59, 72, 98n.21, n.25
Kayne, Richard, 11, 26, 43
Keenan, Edward, 75
Kinande, 112
Kirkpatrick, Charles, 130n.5
Koopman, Hilda, 69
Kroch, Anthony, 90
Ladusaw, Bill, 99n.30
Langendoen, D. Terence, 98n.24, 102n.47
Lasnik, Howard, 5, 13, 18, 29, 53n.19, 57, 73, 96n.2, 106
Lexical government. *See* Head Government
Lexical Relatedness (L-relatedness), and status of relative head, 67
Lightfoot, David, 24-27, 30-31
Local subject extraction, 31; *in situ* analysis, 104, 116, 118-121. *See also* Vacuous Movement Hypothesis (VMH)
Lodge, Ken R., 73, 99n.35
Longobardi, Giuseppe, 51n.8
Maling, Joan, 105
Manner of Speech complements, 41-48, 55n.41; failure of passivization and topicalization with, 54n.37; as selected adjuncts, 42-44; *that*-less examples of, 46-7
Melvold, Janis, 55n.45
Minimality, 109; Relativized, 19, 28, 110, 115.
Müller, Gereon, 13
Naguka, Ruta, 71
Negative Polarity Items (NPIs), in existential sentences, 76-77
NP-*Tns*-VP Filter, 98n.23
Nominative Island Condition, 107
McCawley, James D., 71, 73, 75, 77, 79, 89, 98n.27, 101n.45
McCloskey, Jim, 4, 29, 52n.11, 55n.40, 62, 97n.11, 98n.27, 118-9, 121

McDavid, Virginia, 55n.45
McNally, Louise, 75, 76, 79, 91, 98n.28, 99n.29-31,n.34
Nominative Island Condition (NIC), 107-8
Norwegian, 105, 108
Noun Complement Clauses, 48-50
Null Complementizers (C^0), incorporation of null C^0, 20-24; governed C^0 which cannot be null, 27-31; lexical government at PF, 24-27; proper government requirement, 19-33; ungoverned null C^0, 31-33
Null Determiners, 6, 51n.8
Old English, 105
Papiamentu, 105
Path Containment Condition (PCC), 118n.6, 122n.6
Perlmutter, David, 103, 105, 113, 124n.15
Perlmutter's conjecture, 105, 113
Pesetsky, David, 7, 18, 20-23, 27, 51n.4-5, 52n.9-10,n.17, 54n.36, 103, 106-9, 113, 122n.1, n.3, n.6, 130n.4
Postnominal modifiers, 57, 70; distribution parallels subject contact clauses, 92-95
PP, as subject, 34
Prepositional Complementizers, 29-31
Prince, Ellen, 90-1
Proper Binding Condition, 97n.17
Pseudo relatives, 73-77; analysis of subject contact clauses, 77-81; dissimilar construction in Romance, 98n.26
Pullum, Geoff, 3
Que/qui alternation, 104, 114
Quirk, Randolph, 96n.1
R-Binding, 61
Reduced Relatives. *See* Postnominal modifiers
Reinhart, Tanya, 97n.16
Relativized Minimality. *See* Minimality

Resumptive pronouns, in contact clauses, 93n.15, 101n.43
Right Node Raising (RNR), 24-25
Rizzi, Luigi, 10, 18-19, 31, 53n.22, 85, 97n.11, 104, 110-122, 123n.7, n.8
Roberts, Ian, 97n.11, 121
Rochemont, Michael, 13, 50n.2
Root clauses, category of; 3, 39
Ross, John Robert, 36, 52n.16
Rothstein, Susan D., 32, 53n.26
Safir, Kenneth, 64, 79, 97n.17
Saito, Mamoru, 13, 29, 53n.19
Semantic (S-)selection, 7, 41
Sentence Trace Universal (STU), 35-6, 38
Scandinavian; 5, 118n.7
Small Clause, analysis of existentials, 79; as subject, 37
Smith, Carlota, 53n.25, 57-8, 70, 92
Sobin, Nicholas, 105, 122n.2
Spanish, 111
Sportiche, Dominique, 69
Sternefeld, Wolfgang, 13
Stockwell, Robert, 32, 68, 96n.5
Stowell, Tim, 5, 8, 11, 18, 26, 40, 51n.4, 54n.37, 55n.38, 68, 79, 96n.4, 125
Subject Contact Clauses, 9, 58, 71-95; distribution is limited, 72-3; distribution wider in some dialects, 87-89; explaining restricted distribution of, 89-95; as pseudo-relatives, 77-81; as restrictive relatives, 81-87; as Topic-Comment structures, 100-101n.42
Svenonius, Peter, 25, 52n.11, 53n.18, 54n.32, n.33, 105, 130n.1
Swedish, 111
Swingle, Kari, 25, 52n.14
Swiss German, 123n.7
Taraldsen, Knut Tarald, 105, 107
That-less relatives. *See* Contact clauses

That-trace Effect, 9, 103-122; and IP-hypothesis, 115-121; dialectal variation, 105-106
That-trace Filter, 106
Topic-Comment, and subject contact clauses, 100n.42
Uniformity Requirement on Chains, 36-7
Vacuous Movement Hypothesis (VMH), 10, 118-121
Verbs of 'physical manipulation', 47
Vikner, Sten, 35, 97n.11, 121
Vincent, Nigel, 85, 100n.37
Visser, Fredericus Theodorus, 98n.21
VP-ellipsis, and manner of speech verbs 46, 55n.40
Webelhuth, Gert, 10n.3, 29, 34-8, 40
Weisler, Steven, 10n.3, 96n.3, n.5
West Flemish, 112
Williams, Edwin, 22, 53n.31, 99n.31
Williams, Kemp, 29
Wolfram, Walt, 96n.1
X-Binding, 61
X´-theory, status of S(entence) within, 3-4
Zaenen, Annie, 105
Zero(-comp) relatives. *See* Contact clauses

For Product Safety Concerns and Information please contact our EU
representative GPSR@taylorandfrancis.com
Taylor & Francis Verlag GmbH, Kaufingerstraße 24, 80331 München, Germany

www.ingramcontent.com/pod-product-compliance
Lightning Source LLC
Chambersburg PA
CBHW061841300426
44115CB00013B/2471